Classics
of the
Road

Classics
of the
Road

David Burgess Wise

ORBIS PUBLISHING · London

© Orbis Publishing Limited 1978
ISBN: 0 85613 019 2
Printed in Italy by Poligrafici Calderara

The Mall, London, during the early days of the
General Strike. With only 'pirate' buses running
and no trains at all, it was left to the everyday
man in the street to transport himself, and as
many people as he could get on board, to London. Cars were not just classics but necessities.

Contents

Introduction
by David Burgess Wise

What makes an early car a classic? Some special feature of design or engineering, perhaps, particularly elegant styling or possibly just the sheer eccentricity of its conception. In a way, every car built before the mid 1930s has some feature which distinguishes it as a classic of its type, some unique element which marks it as an individual.

An important factor is that even the humblest cars of that era are the expression of distinct personalities, of engineers who knew exactly what they wanted and who were not prepared to compromise to suit the whims of the marketing man. Even that ubiquitous vehicle, the Model T Ford, was the work of a close-knit trio—Joseph Galamb, Childe Harold Wills and Henry Ford himself—who built their own quirks and foibles into it, to make it a car unlike anything else on the roads—except for the the other sixteen million or so Model Ts built between 1908 and 1927! In the mid 1930s, all that was to change, and the names which came before the public were those of stylists: design was no longer by individual but by committee.

I have driven many cars which can be counted as classics, from an 1898 Georges Richard, a somewhat lame copy of the Benz, with horrifying chain-and-sprocket steering and an almost negative power output, to a 1931 blown 2.3-litre Alfa Romeo which Nuvolari himself raced in the Mille Miglia. Each one of these vehicles had something different to offer—a new driving technique to learn, perhaps, or an extra delicacy of control—which singles it out in the memory as something special. In the following pages are those vehicles from days gone by: not only the extravagant Packards, Rolls-Royces and Hispano-Suizas, but the more eccentric vehicles like the diamond-formation-wheeled Sunbeam-Mabley, the curious air-cooled Phänomobil and the innovative if bulbous little Trojan. To add a contemporary air to the book, some of the cars are shown as they were in the early days, when they were the Ford Escorts, Volkswagen Beetles and Rolls-Royce Camargues of yesteryear. It all adds up to a spirit of individuality which in everyday motoring has disappeared, but which has been brought to you here in *Classics of the Road*.

Progress was at its most rapid in the early days of motoring: the belt-driven 1898 *Orient Express* was crude, unreliable and prone to breakdown, while the 9hp *Peugeot*, only five years its junior, was regarded as a motor car designed for long-distance touring.

(Paul Foulkes Halbard collection)

1892 Peugeot
1897 Panhard & Levassor
1897 Daimler

'The Peugeot firm', wrote the turn-of-the-century French motoring author Gerard Lavergne, 'manufactures various models of fashionable cars'. This ornate vehicle, built in 1892 only two years after Peugeot began production, was very much a one-off, assembled to the order of the Bey of Tunis. Under its rococo styling, however, this was a typical early Peugeot, with a vee-twin Daimler engine of 1018cc mounted at the rear of a tubular chassis through which the cooling water was circulated.

Peugeot's great rival in the 1890s was the firm of Panhard & Levassor, which also used Daimler engines, but mounted at the front of the chassis in a layout which was to become virtually universal for generations of motor cars to come. The car illustrated (bottom) dates from the middle of the decade and is fitted with a Daimler Phönix (Phénix in France) vertical-twin engine of 2.4 litres. Although Panhards made their name in racing, tiller steering was scarcely satisfactory at speed.

One of the more outrageous business empires established in the early days of motoring was that set up by Harry Lawson, with the aim of cornering the British market. Two of the notable companies involved were the Great Horseless Carriage Company and its sibling, the Daimler Motor Company, which, despite its name, built anglicised Panhards (below). This 1897 model has the primitive hot-tube ignition—considered to be more reliable than the electrical variety—although its tiller has been replaced by a wheel.

The year 1899 saw Panhard firmly established as the 'leading marque of the automobile world', and still virtually unbeatable in competition. In that season, the first true racing cars appeared, breaking away from the concept that competition machinery should be merely a more powerful version of the standard touring car. The catalyst was the announcement on 11 April of the longest motor race yet organised, the 2500 kilometre Tour de France, sponsored by *Le Matin*, a paper with a penchant for promoting motoring marathons.

Starting and ending at Paris, the race circled mid-France, taking in Cabourg, Nantes, Périgueux, Vichy, Aix-les-Bains and Nancy, and attracted nineteen starters, eight of which were Panhards. Stray dogs caused several minor accidents, and most of the entrants suffered from mechanical failures of more or less serious nature, but the winning car, this 16hp Panhard driven by the Chevalier René de Knyff, led all the way.

The first truly popular motor car was the little Locomobile steamer, although the frailty of its construction ensured that its vogue was short-lived. This 1902 model (below) belonged to Sir John Dickson Poynder, Bart, MP, a veteran of the Boer War, and whose London estates included large areas around Holborn. The condenser at the front of the car turned the exhaust steam to water, so that the Locomobile would not break the law prohibiting the emission of 'visible vapour'.

Autumn 1899 sees the first Renault cars (bottom). On the left is an 1897 De Dion-engined quadricycle, with Marcel Renault in the passenger seat; in the middle is the prototype Renault voiturette, a $\frac{3}{4}$hp car driven by Louis Renault; and on the right, driven by Paul Hugé, is the first of the more powerful $1\frac{3}{4}$hp models introduced in 1899.

1897 **De Dion-Bouton**
1895 **Cannstatt-Daimler**
1898 **Delahaye**

The most famous and most widely copied of all the early proprietary power units was the De Dion-Bouton single-cylinder engine, here fitted to one of that company's own voiturettes of 1897. Such was the pace of work at the De Dion works at Puteaux, near Paris, that if any engine failed to run properly when bench tested, it was immediately dismantled for spares, this being quicker than searching for and rectifying the fault.

Gottlieb Daimler's first car ran in 1886, but he was primarily interested in developing a universal power unit, and not the overall design of the car. which is why this 1895 Cannstatt-Daimler has such a primitive air (below). In less than ten years, however, Daimler's associate, Maybach, was to be responsible for the design of the Mercédès, 'the car of the day after tomorrow'.

A 'bubbling carburettor' was one of the unusual features of the power unit of this 1898 Delahaye (bottom). Others were a particularly reliable electric ignition system and the fact that no governor was fitted to the engine, at a time when most car builders believed in controlling power units so that they would run at a constant speed. Also, the Delahaye, which has a sound racing pedigree, was fitted with dual exhaust cams, one set for starting and one set for normal running up to a heady 25mph.

1898 Egg
1898 Decauville

Believed to be Switzerland's oldest surviving car, this 1898 Egg (below) was built in Zurich by Rudolf Egg. Like its ecclesiastical namesake, the Egg was 'good in parts': it featured an infinitely variable belt transmission on similar lines to the modern DAF Variomatic, but the differential gear was completely exposed, operating without lubricant or protection. Also, its straight-cut bevel gears must have been fearfully noisy in operation.

Decauville were famed as builders of narrow-gauge railways long before they went into car production. Their first model, which made its debut in 1898, was known as the Voiturelle (right). Despite its fragile appearance, the Voiturelle, which had a primitive form of independent front suspension, was quite a reliable vehicle. In 1900, on the Crystal Palace cycle track in London, a Voiturelle covered 1000 miles almost non-stop.

1895 Rochet-Schneider
1901 Oldsmobile
1899 Panhard & Levassor
1899 Nesselsdorf

Most noted of all the car makers of the French city of Lyon, Rochet-Schneider began production in 1894 with a rear-engined belt-driven model on Benz lines, which was produced until 1901. This splendid *vis-a-vis* (below left), with its Victoria hood, dates from 1895 and has styling very similar to that of the contemporary Peugeot, even down to the handlebar steering.

'Nothing to watch but the road' was the slogan of the world's first mass-production motor-car, the 1901 curved-dash Oldsmobile (top centre). Its layout was basic in the extreme: a slow-running single-cylinder engine under the seat, full-length springs either side which acted as a kind of bouncy chassis frame, two-speed epicyclic gearing and tiller steering. By 1904, output had reached 5000 units a year, a considerable figure for the period.

Commandant Krebs was a director of Panhard & Levassor and the designer of one of the best carburettors of the early days of motoring. The light car he designed in 1899 was, however, a classic of awfulness, combining in its layout just about every solecism of design (bottom centre). Panhard quietly disposed of the manufacturing rights to Clément and it was widely built under licence. Its mechanism, 'worthy of an opium-smoker's delirium', was wont to catch fire at the least provocation.

Although their factory was in the Austro-Hungarian Empire, the Nesselsdorfer Wagenbau-Fabriks-Gesellschaft, founded in the early nineteenth century, were coachbuilders to the Prussian Court as well as makers of railway carriages. They built their first car in 1897, a 5hp four-seater with a Benz flat-twin power unit. Among those concerned in the construction of this vehicle, known as the Prasident, was a young engineer named Hans Ledwinka. In 1899, he designed this racing car for Nesselsdorf, and with it the wealthy

industrialist Theodor von Liebig achieved a number of competition successes in France, Germany and and Austria. In 1923, the Nesselsdorfer company, which now found itself in the new Czech republic, was renamed Tatra.

1900 Georges Richard
1898 Renault
1899 Wolseley

The first car built by Georges Richard, of Ivry-Port, near Paris, was a feeble machine with belt drive, which appeared in 1897. However, by 1900, the company was producing a far more reliable vehicle in the shape of this little voiturette (below), designed by the Vivinus company of Brussels. Belt-driven, with a $3\frac{1}{2}$hp single-cylinder engine, it was one of the liveliest and most refined light cars of its day. The Vivinus was also built under licence in Britain by New Orleans of Twickenham.

In 1898, a wealthy button-maker's son named Louis Renault built himself a light car for amusement, but received so many orders from friends that he decided to put it into production. In the first six months, sixty cars like this one (bottom) were delivered, with 273cc air-cooled De Dion engines—from which Renault carefully chiselled the name—mounted at the front behind a wire-mesh grille. The outstanding feature of the Renault was its shaft-drive transmission.

The Wolseley company were famous manufacturers of sheep-shearing machinery, whose designer, Herbert Austin, had been interested in the horseless carriage since 1894. He built his first car, a two-cylinder three-wheeler, in 1895 and followed it with a single-cylinder machine a year later. His first four-wheeler (below) was constructed in 1899; it competed in the 1900 Thousand Miles Trial and won a silver medal and first prize in its class. It had a horizontal single-cylinder engine which was linked to a three-speed gearbox by a flat belt; final drive was by side chains. Production models followed similar lines, although with chain drive between engine and gearbox. Their success established the Wolseley company as one of the biggest in the British car industry, with an output of 3000 cars a year by 1914.

1899 Daimler
1899 Renault
1901 Arrol-Johnston

Owned by the Hon John Scott-Montagu, father of the present Lord Montagu of Beaulieu, this 1899 Daimler was the first British car to race on the Continent with a British driver. Montagu took third place in the tourist class in the 1899 Paris–Ostend race with this 3-litre, four-cylinder car. In the next year, it won a bronze medal in the Thousand Miles Trial, and by 1902 it was already being described as 'a good old stager', having covered well over 20,000 miles.

In 1899, a more powerful Renault voiturette appeared, with a 1¾hp power unit, again built by De Dion. Now, the wheelbase could be lengthened to take an extra passenger on a spider seat (below). However, Renault had already built a prototype saloon car, a stumpy two-seater which resembled the Holy City in that the length, the height and the breadth of it were equal.

The somewhat ponderous look of the 1901 Arrol-Johnston Dogcart (bottom) can perhaps be understood when it is realised that its promotors were railway engineer George Johnston and Sir William Arrol, designer of the Forth Bridge. However, this Glasgow-built high-wheeler was strong and reliable and well suited to the primitive motoring conditions then existing in Scotland. Its flat-twin power unit had two pistons per cylinder, linked by short connecting rods to rocking levers acting on longer rods which actually

turned the crankshaft; it was started by pulling on a rope which came up through the floorboards. Complex it may have been, but its makers claimed it gave 'silent running, minimum vibration'. There was a six-seater A-J, too, with an extra row of stalls ahead of the driver.

1900 La Va Bon Train
1901 Columbia

The French have always had a genius for producing eccentric vehicles, and MM Larroumet et Lagarde, of Agen, Lot-et-Garonne, were no exception. In 1900, they marketed a De Dion-engined voiturette called La Va Bon Train—'Goes like blazes'–(opposite page) which was midway between a motor tricycle and a light car. Oddly enough, the little town of Agen, famed for its 23-arch aqueduct, was also the home of another strange tricar, La Nef, built in 1901 with an immensely long steering tiller and four seats.

Electric cars enjoyed a short-lived vogue around the turn of the century. One of the most popular was the Columbia, built in Hartford, Connecticut, and sold in Britain as the City & Suburban, where it was popular with 'many well known leaders of society', including Queen Alexandra, who owned the 1901 Victoriette shown on this page. As early as 1902, City & Suburban were operating a garage capable of holding eight hundred cars in a converted skating rink in Westminster.

1900 **Clément-Gladiator**
1901 **FIAT**
1902 **Berna**
1901 **Rochet-Petit**

Neat, light and elegant, the 1900 Clément-Gladiator (below left) is everything that its stablemate, the Clément-Panhard, was not. Power was provided by a 2¼hp De Dion engine geared to the back axle, giving the little car a lively performance. By 1903, the Clément company, whose factory was at Levallois-Perret, Seine, France, had been acquired by Harvey Du Cros, of the English Dunlop company. Its founder, Adolphe Clément, then began producing cars under the name Clément-Bayard.

The Fabbrica Italiana Automobili Torino was founded in 1899, taking over the Ceirano cycle business. At first, FIAT built little 6hp rear-engined voiturettes, but by 1901 they were producing this 1.2-litre twin-cylinder model (centre top) with its engine mounted at the front under a Panhard-style bonnet; it featured chain final drive.

Joseph Wyss of Berne, Switzerland, built his first Berna cars in 1902. This model (bottom left) was on similar lines to the contemporary De Dion-Bouton. It had a 785cc single-cylinder engine mounted at the rear and three-seater coachwork with a 'sideways' front seat. It was no mean achievement to go into production with a motor vehicle in Switzerland, a country in which cars were banned from some cantons and drastically restricted by law in others.

Obscurity, it seems, breeds obscurity in motoring circles, for when the Société Rochet of Paris (not to be confused with Rochet Frères *or* Rochet-Schneider, both from Lyon) decided to go into car production, they chose to build not a well established design but an oddity called the Rossel, whose designer preferred making steam tractors. After a couple of years, a far better car appeared, this little Rochet-Petit, which had a rear-mounted $4\frac{1}{2}$hp Aster engine and four-speed gearbox.

1902 Mors
1901 Sunbeam-Mabley
1901 Baker

Motor racing in the period 1899–1902 was dominated by the French Mors company. This 1902 60hp model, impeccably restored by British collector Bill Lake, is the actual car raced in the 1902 Paris–Vienna event by the Belgian Baron Pierre de Caters, who finished eighteenth out of eighty finishers. On 29 July 1902, at Ostend, De Caters broke the land speed record with this car, becoming the first driver to exceed 75mph over a flying start kilometre.

Mr Mabberley Smith was an architect given to designing large houses in the timbered 'Tudorbethan' idiom, and who fancied himself as a car designer. His first—and hopefully only—design to reach production was the Sunbeam-Mabley, built between 1901 and 1904 by the Sunbeam cycle company. Powered by a $2\frac{3}{4}$hp De Dion engine, which drove the centre pair of wheels, the Sunbeam-Mabley (below right) was steered by the single wheels fore-and-aft (which were out of line). Altogether, it scuttled along the road like a drunken

Victorian sociable settee, and would probably have been better employed as an item of furniture in one of Mr Mabberley Smith's houses . . .

One of the most famous electric cars was the Baker, built in Cleveland, Ohio, between 1899 and 1916. Although this 1901 runabout (bottom) is little more than a battery box on wheels, its designer Walter Baker astounded the motoring world with his record-breaking electric *Torpedo*, announced in 1902. It looked like something out of Jules Verne, with the crew sitting in tandem under a conning tower on top of a wickedly pointed body. It reached over 70mph before it crashed . . .

Henry Hewetson, a London merchant, claimed to have imported the first car into Britain—a Benz—in 1894. Subsequently, he formed a company to handle the British agency for the make. In 1902, Hewetson, in the trilby hat, decided to drive a Benz 100 miles a day for three months. With him in the car is Lord Kingsburgh, Lord Justice Clerk of Scotland and a keen pioneer motorist. As this Benz had the new-fangled pneumatic tyres on the front wheels. Hewetson was accompanied by a sixteen-year-old named St John Nixon (later a famous motoring historian) on a motor cycle who repaired the tyres when they punctured. For all his experience, Hewetson could not mend a punctured tyre . . .

The British Royal Family were enthusiastic pioneer motorists—even the octogenarian Duke of Cambridge enjoyed a ride in the passenger seat of that dangerous device, the Bollée tricar—and one of their favourite marques was the British Daimler. Here, Princess Henry of Battenburg, with Prince Alexander and Princess Ena (who, a couple of years later, was to marry that motorphile monarch, Alfonso XIII of Spain), is seen on a 22hp Daimler in the Hampshire village of Buckler's Hard, on the Montagu Estate (below).

Alfred Harmsworth, later Lord Northcliffe, founder of the *Daily Mail*, was a fervent advocate of fast and powerful motor cars, with a horrendous annual tyre bill to prove it. This was one of his more unusual cars, a Mercédès-Mixte of 1903, in which the engine generated electricity to drive motors built into the front hubs. It was one of the first successful designs of the young Dr Ferdinand Porsche, and was probably the earliest production car to have electric starting (bottom).

1903 Mercédès
1903 Thornycroft
1903 Mercédès

'See the Mercédès, shapeless, unpaintable . . . ' warbled the one-legged Edwardian poet W.E. Henley. However, the Mercédès car was one of the handsomest vehicles of its day—and one of the fastest. In November 1902, Mercédès introduced their new 60hp model, with a 9¼-litre, four-cylinder, bi-block engine. In the following year, a stripped '60' (below) cost over £2000, but offered 70mph-plus performance at a time when the British speed limit was only 12mph. Its smaller contemporary, the

18/22hp Mercédès (right), was less fierce, with an engine of just over 3 litres. In 1903, *The Autocar* tested a 'dainty white eighteen', commenting that the quiet running engine could be 'compared to nothing else but the ticking of a somewhat robust eight-day clock'.

John I. Thornycroft was a steam-launch builder on the River Thames who had built an experimental steam carriage in the mid nineteenth century and who later pioneered the steam-powered commercial vehicle. His first venture into petrol vehicles came in 1903 with a range of cars which included this 20hp, four-cylinder model of 3628cc (left), which was offered with the advanced feature of a belt-driven dynamo to charge the ignition batteries.

1903 Prunel
1903 Cadillac

The Prunel company, of Puteaux, Seine, were in production from 1900 to 1907, during which time they managed to build 'pleasure cars and chassis, motor-omnibus chassis (single & double deck), lorries, delivery vans, etc, etc'. This 1903 two-seater was one of their smaller models, although Prunel did subsequently offer cars up to 40/50hp. In 1905, comedian Will Evans ran a 12hp two-cylinder Prunel, expressing himself 'more than delighted . . . with the magnificent way in which it acted'.

In March 1903, Henry Ford resigned from the Henry Ford Company (founded in 1901 to exploit his designs), determined to seek his independence. Bereft of their figurehead, the company reorganised and called itself 'Cadillac', after Antoine of that ilk, founder of Detroit in 1701. The first Cadillac model was designed by Ford and improved by the company's engineer, Henry M. Leland, who built its one-cylinder engine to a high standard.

1901 Ceirano
1903 Lorraine-Dietrich
1903 White

Between them, the three Ceirano brothers—Giovanni Battista, Giovanni and Matteo—seemed to have fathered the Italian motor industry. Giovanni Battista's first company was acquired by Giovanni Agnelli and became FIAT, after which he sold Agnelli's cars for a while. Then, in company with his brother Matteo, he set up the Ceirano Company in Turin in 1901 building a 5hp car (below) based on the Renault. It used a 600cc single-cylinder power unit imported from France.

Dating from around 1905, this racing Lorraine-Dietrich 45hp (bottom left) was one of the first examples to be fitted with the characteristic 'shouldered' radiator, bearing the Cross of Lorraine, which distinguished the marque in Edwardian days. Earlier models were just known as De Dietrich.

'Incomparable' was the adjective applied by its makers to the White steam car, first built in 1900 by the White Sewing Machine Company of Cleveland, Ohio, and unique among its contemporaries in having a semi-flash boiler with virtually automatic control. The first Whites were fairly basic steam buggies, but in 1903 the design matured into a wheel-steered tonneau with a 10hp compound engine, powerful enough to carry limousine bodywork.

1903 Humber
1903 De Dietrich
1903 De Dietrich

Thomas Humber was famed as a bicycle builder long before his first car appeared in 1896. The company had by then become part of Harry J. Lawson's dubious motor monopoly, and the first powered vehicles did nothing to enhance the firm's reputation. Reformed as an independent company in 1900, Humber were soon building some excellent light cars, one of the best being the little 5hp Humberette single-cylinder model introduced in 1903, the first Humber to be built in large numbers. Early Humbers had two unique features: a single-spoke steering wheel and the fact that their engines cranked anti-clockwise, a feature claimed to reduce the risk of a broken wrist in case of a backfire when starting.

A company with even earlier origins than Humber was the French De Dietrich firm, founded in 1684, which in 1896 acquired the manufacturing rights to a design by Amédée Bollée fils of Le Mans. This Bollée-Dietrich was the first petrol car to have a shaft-driven rear axle (although primary drive was by belts), but the design which replaced it in 1900 was chain-driven, and originated with the Marseillaise firm of Turcat-Méry. The two cars shown on this page are both 24hp De Dietrichs designed by Turcat-Méry, and built in 1903. The upper vehicle was fitted with a racing body by the late Richard Shuttleworth, while the lower one was rediscovered in the 1960s after being stored for many decades and subsequently restored to its now beautiful condition.

1903 Siddeley
1903 FIAT
1904 Peerless

Although it bore the name of Siddeley, this 1903 twin-cylinder tonneau was no more than a slightly modified Peugeot. Nor was its stablemate any more original, for the 6hp single-cylinder model was built by Wolseley, and fitted with a Siddeley radiator. This loose union between the two companies became a marriage of convenience in 1905, when Wolseley absorbed Siddeley. John Davenport Siddeley became manager of the new consortium, however.

Clearly inspired by contemporary Mercédès practice, the 1903 16/24hp FIAT had a four-cylinder engine cast in two pairs and low-tension magneto ignition (below); it was the work of FIAT's new designer, Ing Enrico. The main difference between this car and the Mercédès was that the FIAT used a wooden chassis strengthened with steel flitch plates, while Mercédès frames were always of pressed steel.

The Peerless company, of Cleveland, Ohio, still exists today as the brewer of Carlings Ale, but in the years from 1900 to 1931, Peerless built some of America's finest luxury cars. This model (bottom) is a 1904 24hp tourer, which cost $4250 complete with canopy and glass windscreen, then regarded very much as extras. Its designer was Louis P. Mooers, one of the first to incorporate lessons learned on the race track into production vehicles.

1904 Wolseley
1905 Cameron

This 6hp single-cylinder Wolseley (below), dating from 1904, was designed by Herbert Austin. Like all production Wolseleys built while Austin was manager, it had a horizontal engine. Austin obstinately refused to have anything to do with the high-speed vertical engine which, he claimed, was difficult to lubricate, thus wearing out quickly. Ironically, Wolseley crankshafts themselves were prone to embarrassing failure and the public thought the car old-fashioned, anyway.

The odd little car on the opposite page is a Cameron 9hp runabout, dating from around 1905, which was produced by the third incarnation of one of the most frequently reorganised companies in the history of the motor car. The first Cameron cars were built in 1902 by the United Motor Company of Pawtucket, Rhode Island, USA, and thereafter there were another seven 'Cameron' companies and factories before the marque finally sank from view in 1919.

1905 Ford
1906 Cadillac
1904 FIAT
1904 Brushmobile
1904 Franklin
1906 Pope-Toledo

Styling soon became an important factor in selling motor cars and, when it became fashionable for automobiles to have bonnets, the makers of underfloor-engined gas buggies followed the style. Neither of the two cars shown on the far left has an engine under its bonnet, just oil and fuel tanks. The upper photograph shows a 15hp twin-cylinder Ford Model F of 1905, while the lower picture is of a 1906 single-cylinder Cadillac.

'The Marvel of 1904' was how the British concessionaires described this 16/21hp FIAT (below), which was the very car exhibited at the Cordingley Motor Show in March 1904; the body style is known as 'Shrewsbury Phaeton', with access to the back seats being gained by swinging the front passenger seat forwards like a door. Already, the British agents were finding the capitalised name of FIAT too clumsy, and familiarising it to 'Fiat'.

Aura vincit—'Air Conquers'—was the the motto of the Franklin company of Syracuse, New York, who, from their birth in 1901 to the end of production in 1934, built nothing but air-cooled cars. This 1904 model (below right) has a 12hp transverse-four engine, and is identical to the car in which L.L. Whitman halved the trans-America record to 33 days in 1904, averaging 155 miles a day, even over deserts. Although travel-stained . . . the car gave little evidence of the ordeal', stated a contemporary report of the event.

The American Colonel Albert Pope ran a complex business empire but, of all the marques under his control, the finest was the Pope-Toledo, with its distinctive peaked radiator, of the 1903–1909 period. The 1906 Type 12 Pope-Toledo (bottom) had a four-cylinder 35/40hp engine with 'planetic' cooling, could seat seven and sold for $3700 fully equipped and painted to the customer's specification.

The little blue car shown left is a curious survivor, being the sole known example of the 6hp Brushmobile of 1904. Its engine and chassis (which had coil springing all round) were built by Vauxhall for Brush, an electrical engineering company which produced cars between 1902 and 1904. The bodywork was apparently 'modernised' around 1912, as light cars did not have side doors in 1904.

This was the very first Napier car to be built, early in 1900. Owned by Edward Kennard, it was, however, driven by S.F. Edge in the Thousand Miles' Trial of 1900, an event intended 'to prove . . . that the motor car is, even in its present state of development, a serious and trustworthy means of locomotion; not a toy dangerous and troublesome alike to the public and its owner'. Despite minor troubles like the carburettor breaking in two, this 8hp twin-cylindered car came first in its class and second overall in the whole Trial.

Originally published around 1900 in the magazine *Les Sports Modernes,* this illustration (left) shows the 5cv Decauville Voiturette as it appeared when new. But one wonders whether the fashionable ladies would have looked so well turned out after a few kilometres in the Decauville which, despite its independent front suspension, was totally devoid of any form of springing at the rear.

The young King Alfonso XIII of Spain and his Queen loved nothing better than to tour their country by car, preferably a high-powered machine like this Daimler of *circa* 1906 vintage (below). 'Many stories are told of the Young King of Spain's pranks *en automobile*', wrote one Everard Digby in 1906. 'The stately grandees of his court are horrified at the idea of their king tearing about the country at forty miles an hour, to find out for himself what he wants to know about his people . . . he shares the accidents of the road with the humblest motorist in the land, and takes them with the good nature of a true sportsman.'

1905 Delaunay-Belleville
1905 Peugeot
1906 Rover

Delaunay-Belleville of St Denis-sur-Seine were renowned makers of steam boilers and steam engines long before they introduced their first car to the public at the beginning of 1905. The round radiator and bonnet of the Delaunay-Belleville recalled the company's marine associations, and one of the marque's outstanding features was full pressure lubrication of the engine bearings, at a time when most makers relied on crude 'faith, hope and gravity' systems.

Peugeot were ironmongers and makers of corset stays before they turned to cycle manufacture over ninety years ago. A Serpollet-designed steamer was built in 1889, but soon the firm had taken up the petrol car. From rear-engined vehicles on cycle lines, the company had progressed to building cars on Mercédès lines by 1902. However, they had not forgotten their origins, and included in the 1902 range was a somewhat basic motor quadricycle which sold at £110 in Britain. This (below) is a 1905 example.

The first production model from the Rover company was a little 8hp single-cylinder model, designed by E.W. Lewis, which appeared in 1904. In its original form, the 8hp Rover used a backbone chassis in which engine, clutch, gearbox, prop-shaft housing and rear axle formed a single unit, the rear of the body being sprung to the chassis. Later models used a more conventional chassis (bottom) and were built until 1912.

1906 Delahaye
1906 Ford
1906 De Dion-Bouton

According to one writer, the Type 32 Delahaye (below left) was 'absolutely unbreakable'. Certainly, its 1944cc engine was called on to cope with quite massive coachwork, like the *limousine de voyage* shown here, which it did with silence and smoothness. In 1910, the young Parry Thomas—to achieve fame in the 1920s as a racing driver as well as an engineer—used a Type 32 Delahaye as a test bed for his ingenious electric transmission.

In 1906, at the insistence of his backers, Henry Ford built his first luxury car, the Model K Ford (bottom left). It was fast but fragile, the two-speed epicyclic transmission being inadequate to deal with the torque of a 6-litre, six-cylinder engine. It did not sell well, and was soon dropped, leaving Ford to pursue his vision of 'building a car for the multitudes'.

For 1906, De Dion-Bouton announced a new 8hp single-cylinder model, with a pressed-steel chassis (replacing the tubular construction of earlier types) and a sliding-pinion, three-speed gear in unit with the back axle instead of the clash-proof two-speed, expanding-clutch transmission which had become associated with the marque. However, coupé coachwork such as that shown below was still uncommon on so small a car.

1906 Stanley
1907 Gladiator
1907 De Dion-Bouton

Perhaps the most famous make of steam car ever built was the Stanley, produced in Massachussetts until 1927 by the Stanley twins, Francis E. and Freelan O. The 1906 Model EX (left) is a particularly interesting example, representing a transitional stage between the earlier steam buggies and the fast and famous Stanley Steamers of latter years. Although this car has its boiler at the front under a rounded bonnet, it retains the old side-tiller steering.

Dating from 1907, this 12/14hp Gladiator (below) was built in Le Pré-St Gervais, France. Its pressed-steel chassis seems to have been an option only available on the British market (where this model sold for £375), for the home market, apparently, had to make do with flitch-plated wood chassis on their Gladiators.

Another early example of closed coachwork on a De Dion-Bouton chassis (left), this time on a twin-cylinder model dating from 1907. Extra cylinders were a big bonus for De Dion owners, it seems, sparing the driver 'the necessity of manipulating individual levers under normal conditions', according to the handbook.

1907 Clément-Bayard
1908 Züst
1908 Sizaire-Naudin
1907 Lancia
1908 Darracq

In 1907, the Clément-Bayard company, under the direction of M Guillemon, introduced a 1.6-litre, 10/12hp model, with the advanced feature of a monobloc engine in unit with the gearbox (below). It had a dashboard radiator and 'coal-scuttle' bonnet, which were to remain features of this marque until 1914.

During the first decade of this century, several manufacturers marketed three-cylinder cars, including Panhard and Vauxhall. The configuration was intended to give smooth running due to the cranks being at 180°. Another three-cylinder model was the 1908 Züst, built in Brescia, Italy (bottom left), with a 1495cc power unit. This model was widely used as a taxi, hence the double-dropped chassis for low step height.

'New ideas are plentiful in this little car,' commented the Press about the Sizaire-Naudin voiturette introduced in 1905 (bottom centre). These ideas included independent front suspension and a rear axle which gave three forward speeds and reverse through the medium of a crown wheel and four pinions of different diameters, moving both laterally and longitudinally (but far from silently . . .).

Son of a wealthy soup manufacturer, Vincenzo Lancia had been both engineer and racing driver before he began car manufacture in 1906 (although a fire at his factory held up production until late 1907). The first production Lancia was the 18/24hp, which later became known as the 2.5-litre Alpha (below). There was a sports roadster version of this model, the 'Lampo', which won America's Savannah Small Car Race in 1908.

Italian by adoption was the little 8/10 hp Darracq (bottom right), built under licence in Milan between 1906 and 1909. A neat little car, with a single-cylinder engine of 1100cc, this French-designed voiturette was the progenitor of one of Italy's most famous marques. Italian sales of Darracqs were poor, the branch factory was closed and replaced by a new company, the Anonima Lombardo Fabbrica Automobili—ALFA for short—which in 1914 became Alfa Romeo, named after its owner, Nicola Romeo.

1908 **Star**
1908 **Rolland-Pilain**
1908 **Adams**
1909 **Stearns**
1908 **Franklin**

As early as the year 1883, Star of Wolverhampton were building cycles and, by the outbreak of the World War I, they were among the six largest motor manufacturers in Britain. During their 35 years of car building, Star turned out a bewildering variety of vehicles, from the first Star-Benz of 1897 to the 1931 Comet and Planet models, claimed to be ten years ahead of their time. Shown here (below) is the 2549cc Star 12 of 1908.

Dating from 1908, this sporting Rolland-Pilain has a 2.1-litre, four-cylinder engine, and is styled on similar lines to the team of Rolland-Pilains which competed—with a total lack of success—in the 1908 Grand Prix des Voiturettes. In 1909, this car, now on display at the Rochetaillée Museum near Lyon, took second place in its class in the Mont Ventoux hill-climb (bottom left).

Like the Model T Ford, the Bedford-built Adams had a foot-operated epicyclic transmission—'Pedals to Push, That's All' was its slogan—but there the resemblance ended. Despite its conventional appearance, the 1908 Adams (below) had a single-cylinder engine under the front seat, the body hinging up to give access. Along with Herbert Austin, the Adam's American designer, Edward R. Hewitt, had helped Sir Hiram Maxim build a gigantic steam-powered aeroplane, which *nearly* flew in 1894.

Identified by the white line around its radiator shell, the Stearns from Cleveland, Ohio (bottom centre), was one of America's finest cars. Shown here is the 1909 Light Tourer which, with a six-cylinder, 12.913cc power unit, was capable of touring at over over 60mph, a fantastic performance for its day. The Stearns marque survived until 1930.

In 1905, Franklin introduced a new range of air-cooled cars, with in-line power units replacing the old transverse engines. The copper cooling fins were cast into the steel cylinders for good heat dissipation, and both four and six-cylinder engines were offered. The four-cylinder engine was used on this brougham (bottom right), which dates from 1908.

George Baldwin Selden claimed he had invented the motor car in 1877, and in the first decade of this century the Association of Licenced Automobile Manufacturers attempted to gain a monopoly in the American motor industry by prosecuting all those who were said to have infringed the Selden 'master patent'. Henry Ford refused to join the ALAM, and was duly taken to court. His engineers built this car, powered by a copy of the engine which J.J. Etienne Lenoir had used in his 1863 motor carriage, and it ran a great deal better than the crude machine which Selden had built to prove the validity of his 1877 design, which up to that point had remained firmly on paper. Ford won the case in 1911, establishing himself as a folk hero in the eyes of the American public.

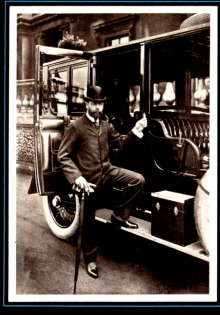

The running-boards of stately landaulettes seem to have been designed specifically for public figures to strike attitudes on . . . although striking platitudes were really the stock-in-trade of David Lloyd George (left) who employed all the eloquence he had learned in his Welsh lawyer's practice when he entered Liberal politics. George V (far left) became King in 1910, when this picture was taken. At that time, all the King's horsepower consisted of four Daimler cars, a Daimler shooting brake and a Leyland lorry. When the King went to Balmoral, the six vehicles travelled up to Scotland aboard a specially built train.

Jack Johnson, then heavyweight boxing champion of the world, photographed around 1910 at the wheel of a 50hp Austin, reputedly that which Dario Resta raced in the 1908 French Grand Prix at Dieppe (although as Resta's car was chain-driven, this seems unlikely, and the car is more probably the live-axled Warwick Wright). Johnson bought the car from Austin after the race and used it for a tour of Europe. The 'out-of-doors' foot-throttle must have made driving this car a draughty business.

1909 Humber
1909 Pierce-Arrow
1909 Turicum

The 8hp Humber introduced during 1908 was a well engineered twin-cylinder light car with a 1527cc engine, capable of cruising at 35mph and returning 28mpg. An advanced feature of the specification was the use of detachable artillery wheels, and the car was excellent value for money, being only £195. However, the model went out of production in 1910. This particular car dates from 1909, and belongs to the National Motor Museum.

The George N. Pierce Company, of Buffalo, New York, built bicycles and birdcages before starting car production in 1901 with a 2¾hp De Dion-engined Motorette. In 1909, using the name of their most successful model, the company became known as Pierce-Arrow, at which time their entire production consisted of six-cylinder cars (below right), of 36hp (5686cc), 48hp (7243cc) and 66hp (10,619cc).

Christened with the ancient name of Zurich, in which it was built from 1904 to 1914, the Turicum car was characterised throughout its production life by the use of friction drive. However, the first couple of Turicums had one feature, which thankfully was not continued on subsequent models—they were *foot*-steered, by twin pedals. This 1909 twin-cylinder car (bottom right) was one of their more ephemeral models, being produced during that season alone.

1909 **Rochet-Schneider**
1911 **Hansa**
1910 **Armstrong-Whitworth**

Looking rather like a Turkish bath on wheels, this 1909 Rochet-Schneider's bodywork (below) is actually patterned on the contemporary hansom cab. Odd though the styling looks nowadays, with its flap-up windscreen and multipaned side windows, in its day it was thought *le dernier cri* for the fashionable Edwardian motorist about town.

A real Edwardian 'boy-racer', the 7/20hp Hansa Type B had a four-cylinder engine with overhead valves, and was capable of some 50mph flat out. An aggressively raked bonnet and flared wings all contributed to the appeal of this model (bottom left), which was the star attraction of Hansa's stand at the 1911 Berlin Motor Show. Despite its sporting image, the Hansa won more prizes for styling than for competition success.

The Newcastle-upon-Tyne engineering company of Armstong-Whitworth began car production in 1904 with the Wilson-Pilcher, which had a preselector gearbox. They first built cars under their own name in 1906, and these were solid, well designed vehicles on conventional lines. By 1910, when the Three-Quarter Landaulette on this page was built, Armstong-Whitworth were offering a monobloc engine with pressure lubrication. In 1919, they merged with Siddeley-Deasy of Coventry.

1910 Bianchi
1910 Renault

Edoardo Bianchi was a Milanese cycle manufacturer who went into car production with a single-cylinder voiturette in 1899. Ten years later, Bianchi had become one of Italy's more notable marques, building solid, reliable cars to the design of Giuseppe Merosi. In 1909, they introduced a big 5-litre, 20/30hp model, with pair-cast cylinders and chain drive. By the time this landaulette (below left) appeared in 1910, shaft drive had been adopted for the 20/30.

One of the most famous Renault light cars was the Type AX, introduced in 1906. Thousands were built, and it was the AX chassis which was used for the Parisian taxis with which General Galliéni was able to rush French troops up to the front line in the Battle of the Marne and turn the German advance on Paris. This particular AX has a 1060cc, twin-cylinder engine (later examples had a 1204cc power unit), and dates from 1910.

1910 Swift

Even in the golden age of motoring, some cars were not all that they seemed, and this little 1910 7hp Austin was one of them, for it was not really Austin at all, but a Swift! Built in the Coventry factory of the Swift Motor Company, but fitted with an Austin radiator, it had a 1087cc, single-cylinder engine, and sold for £150. Around the same time, Austin were also assembling Gladiators for the British market, thus complicating matters still further . . .

1911 **Rolls-Royce**
1911 **Empire**
1912 **Arrol-Johnston**
1912 **Trojan**
1912 **Darracq**

Like Henry Ford, Henry Royce achieved his greatest fame by adhering to a policy of producing just one model for the span of nineteen years. In Royce's case, the car was the 40/50hp Rolls-Royce, first announced in 1906. Initially, the 40/50hp (familiarly known as the 'Silver Ghost', after the thirteenth car of this type) had a 7036cc, six-cylinder engine, but in 1909 the swept volume was raised to 7428cc. This 1911 40/50 (below) has touring coachwork by Barker & Co.

Known as the 'Little Aristocrat', the Empire 20hp car was built in Indianapolis (bottom left). Like so many American cars, it made use of proprietory components, such as a four-cylinder bi-block GBS engine. Open raceabout bodywork, such as that shown here, was fashionable wear on many American chassis of this period. In 1912, production of Empire cars was shifted from Indianapolis to Greenville, Pennsylvania.

Most popular model built by Arrol-Johnston in the Edwardian period was the 15.9hp, which was launched in 1909, the first fruit of a new design policy headed by the firm's new manager T.C. Pullinger, formerly with Sunbeam. The 15.9 had its radiator behind the engine *à la* Renault and, in its original form, pioneered the use of front wheel brakes. However, these proved unsatisfactory and, by the time that the 1912 models (bottom centre) appeared, they had been discarded.

This rotund little car (below) is the prototype of one of the most distinctive designs ever put into quantity production, the Trojan. With a duplex two-stroke engine (whose vee-shaped connecting rods flexed to and fro as they went about their business), solid tyres and cantilever 'wondersprings', the Trojan was Leslie Hounsfield's vision of a car for 'Everyman'. 'It's weird but it goes!' was how he summarised his brainchild; production did not start until 1922, some ten years later.

In 1912, Alexandre Darracq announced that the new models from his factory at Suresnes would be fitted with the Henriod 'valveless' engine (which in fact had more valve than conventional power units, as a rotating valve shaft, connecting inlet and exhaust passages alternately with a single port per cylinder, was employed). The Henriod engine proved gutless and liable to seize irrevocably; poppet-valve models (bottom right) saved the day.

1912 Nazzaro
1912 Fiat
1912 Hispano-Suiza
1912 Opel

Racing driver Felice 'Lucky' Nazzaro enjoyed less than his usual good fortune when he became a car manufacturer in 1912. Unlike his erstwhile team-mate Vincenzo Lancia, Nazzaro found that his sporting reputation was not sufficient to sell cars, and sales remained disappointing during the marque's decade of existence. Most Nazzaro cars were distinctly staid in appearance, and it is likely that this 1912 model once bore far more sober raiment than it does today (below).

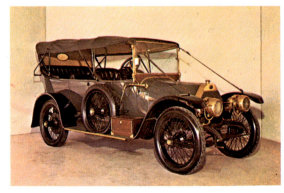

Italian sporting torpedo *par excellence* (bottom left), the 1912 Fiat Tipo 54 had a 5.7-litre, monobloc four-cylinder engine and shaft drive; it sold in Britain at £650 in chassis form, to which coachwork such as that shown here would add another £200 or so. The wire wheels fitted to this car are not standard, for the original specification called for the wooden-spoked artillery type.

Although the Hispano-Suiza company was founded in Barcelona in 1904, seven years later they were building cars in Paris as well. Most famous of all the Edwardian Hispanos was the sporting Alfonso XIII (named after the marque's most prestigious customer), which in its most common form had a long-stroke 3.6-litre engine. The 1912 Alfonso illustrated here (bottom centre) still bears a bullet mark on its steering wheel, where its owner was killed in the Irish troubles of that time.

It was a blessing in disguise when the Opel factory at Russelsheim, Germany, burned down in 1911, for the holocaust enabled the Opel brothers to rebuild in the most modern fashion. By 1912, they were back in production with a bewildering range which started with the basic 1-litre 5/12hp and went up through another seven distinct types—6/16hp (below), 8/20hp, 10/25hp, 14/30hp, 18/40hp, 24/50hp and 34/65hp—to the massive 10.2-litre 40/100hp, priced at £800 in chassis form.

1912 Renault
1913 Metz
1912 Scout
1913 De Dion-Bouton

Alongside his popular twin-cylinder models, Louis Renault also produced some excellent four-cylinder cars such as this 1912 2120cc Type FK, which sold at a chassis price of £272 (below). There were even a couple of big sixes in the pre-World War I lineup—the larger of them, the 37.2hp, growing even bigger after the Armistice, thus becoming the famous 9.1-litre '45', which was produced until 1928, the last survivor of the 'Jurassic Age' of the motor car.

Charles H. Metz was an American engineer with an original line in sales technique. Figuring that there were many amateur mechanics who wanted but could not afford a motor car, he conceived the idea of selling a car to them literally in instalments. The components of the car were separated into fourteen groups, and the prospective motorist bought one group at a time until he had a complete Metz. Later cars like this 1913 Torpedo Runabout (bottom left) came fully assembled, however.

One of the more esoteric British makes of the pre World War I days was the Scout, built by Dean and Burden Brothers of Salisbury, Wiltshire. Although Scouts were available from 1904 to 1923, sales were mostly restricted to the Salisbury area. One of the few occasions on which Scout ranged outside its parochial boundaries was in 1905, when a Scout tourer took ninth place in the Isle of Man Tourist Trophy Race. The car illustrated (below) is a 1912 12/14hp, four-cylinder model.

A direct competitor of the Renault FK was this little De Dion-Bouton (bottom), with a 12hp four-cylinder engine, selling at a chassis price of of £283 in 1913. Already De Dion were past their peak, however, and Renault were in the ascendant. In 1913, Renault sales passed the 10,000 mark for the first time, giving the company 20% of the French market. Well built though the De Dion was, it could not meet that kind of competition.

The first Dodge model to be produced was this 1914 3½-litre tourer (below), photographed here with John and Horace Dodge, who had made their fortune supplying chassis and components to Ford before setting up their own factory at Hamtramck, Detroit. An unusual feature of the Dodge car was its electric starter, which automatically cranked the engine should it stall with the ignition on. Within two years, the Dodge company was the fourth biggest in the American motor industry.

Motor manufacturing entered a new era in 1913, when Henry Ford introduced the moving production line at his Highland Park, Detroit, factory (bottom). The time taken to assemble a car dropped from hours to minutes, giving Ford an unassailable lead in the popular car market for many years. One result of the moving production line was the announcement that Ford cars would be available only in black paint, as the primitive spray equipment was unable to cope with colour changes.

In a scene from a long-forgotten silent melodrama, film star Mary Maclaren climbs aboard a 1915 V8 Cadillac, watched by the envious eyes of the equine set. Cadillac were so confident of the reliability of the electric starting, lighting and ignition system used on their cars that they did not fit a starting handle, and blanked off the aperture where it would normally be inserted.

1913 Argyll
1913 Napier
1913 Ford

The Scottish firm of Argyll operated from a vast terra-cotta factory at Alexandria, just north of Glasgow, although their output never matched the building's potential. Their 1912 models offered technological refinements unique to this marque: single-sleeve valve engines and efficient four-wheel brakes. The 1913 15/30hp Streamline Limousine (left) carries Argyll's own coachwork.

In 1912, S.F. Edge, the ebullient Australian whose marketing genius had made the Napier one of the most fashionable cars of the Edwardian era, quarrelled with Montagu Napier and retired from the motor industry to breed pigs in Sussex, bearing a 'golden handshake' of over £160,000. Napier was an engineer, not a salesman and, under his leadership, the company declined. When this 30/35hp Napier six (below) was built in 1913, sales had fallen to 551 from the 1911 peak of 801.

This 1913 variant of the Model T Ford (left) was known as the Commercial Runabout in America, as its rear seat hinged forward into its footwell to form a flat luggage deck. That rear seat's solitary isolation earned it the nickname 'Mother-in-law seat'.

1913 GN
1913 Lancia
1913 Peugeot

This lethal-looking device (below left) is a 1913 Grand Prix GN cyclecar, the ancestor of the vintage Frazer Nash. It has a 90° GN vee-twin engine (whose elegant induction pipes were adapted cycle handlebars) set in an ash chassis and driving the rear wheels via a two-speed chain-and-dog transmission, through belts and pulleys. It also has cable-and-bobbin steering, a feature which, combined with rather nebulous braking, made the 60mph top speed an exciting prospect . . .

Lancia's Theta of 1913 (bottom left) was their first truly successful design, which incorporated as standard electric lighting and starting, a unique luxury at that date. It also had full pressure lubrication of the engine which, rated at 30hp, had a swept volume of 4.9 litres. In 1913, the fully equipped Theta chassis sold in London for £575; total Theta output was 1696 cars.

In 1911, Ettore Bugatti, newly established as an independent motor manufacturer in Molsheim, Alsace (then still part of Germany), designed an ultra-light four-cylinder car whose engine displaced only 850cc. He offered the licence to manufacture to two companies— Wanderer of Chemnitz, Saxony, and Peugeot, of Beaulieu, France. The latter firm acquired the manufacturing rights, and produced the car as the Bébé Peugeot (below), building 3000 between 1912 and 14.

1913 Fiat
1913 Itala
1913 Vauxhall

Smallest of Fiat's immediately pre-World War I range was the 10/15hp Tipo 51 ('Zero'), which had a 1874cc, four-cylinder engine of remarkably modern appearance and which sold for only £300 in chassis form. 'Cheapness is one thing and inexpensiveness is another', commented Fiat's London agents, and certainly there was nothing skimpy about Tipo 51. Italy was not then the keen market for small cars that it is today, however, and only 2000 or so Zeros were built in three years (1912-15).

Itala of Turin made their name with their competition successes in the first decade of this century—notably their victory in the arduous Pekin—Paris race of 1907, in which year they also had a British assembly plant at Brooklands. Their range became over-complex, however—there was even a venture into rotary-valve engines—and the company never regained their former glory. This is a 1913 25/35hp, 5401cc tourer (below).

Fined for speeding in 1913, W.H. Berry pleaded in mitigation that 'The speedometer was out of action, but the springing was so luxurious, the engine so powerful and quiet . . . that I was not aware that the speed of the car was in excess of 15mph'. That was quite a tribute to what was, after all, a sports car capable of 80mph, the Prince Henry Vauxhall (bottom), which was designed by Laurence Pomeroy. This 1913 two-seater has a 3971cc engine developing 75bhp.

1914 Pilain
1914 Stellite
1913 Daimler

François Pilain of Lyon was the uncle of Emile, the 'Pilain' half of Rolland-Pilain, and had started in the motor industry as early as 1890, when he worked for Serpollet in Paris, building steam cars. He founded the Société des Automobiles Pilain in 1902, building a series of vehicles which were noted for their advanced engineering. This 2-litre Pilain was built in 1914 (below). François had by now quarrelled with his backers and set up another company, to make front-wheel-drive cars.

Like Wolseley, the Electric and Ordnance Accessories Company of Birmingham were a subsidiary of Vickers, and specialised in the manufacture of axles, hubs and roller bearings before adding car manufacture to their repertoire in 1913. Costing £157 10s in two-seater form, their Wolseley-designed Stellite light car used an 1100cc four-cylinder monobloc engine in an armoured-wood chassis, with a two-speed transmission (bottom).

Thanks to their 'Silent Knight'
sleeve-valve engines, Daimlers of the
'teens and 'twenties offered smooth,
silent and slightly smoky progress
and, thanks to early Royal patronage,
the marque enjoyed a particular
cachet with Society, with their list of
customers reading like a digest of
Debrett. This elegant three-quarter
landaulette was known as the
Cranmore, and had a 4.9-litre, six-
cylinder power unit. Daimler were
one of the few luxury car makers to
build their own bodies.

1914 Turner
1914 Sigma
1914 Stutz
1914 Le Zèbre

Turner of Wolverhampton originally built the Belgian Miesse steam car under licence, and persisted with steam until 1913. They had already seen which way the wind of fashion was blowing, however, and introduced their first petrol car in 1906. After a three-year hiatus, they returned to internal combustion in 1911 with a cyclecar, but soon progressed to better things like this 1914 12/20hp (below), with its sporting vee-radiator and detachable-rim wire wheels.

Built in Levallois-Perret, France, between 1913 and 1928, the Sigma was a typical light car of its day, assembled from proprietary parts like Malicet et Blin chassis and Ballot engines. Post-war models also used the CIME engine, and there was an ephemeral twin-cylinder Sigma. This Ballot-engined example (bottom) dates from 1914.

They called the Stutz 'The car that made good in a day' because of its first-time-out eleventh placing in the 1911 Indianapolis 500-mile race. Most famous of all the Stutzes was the 1914 Bearcat speedster, a 'racy creation' which was the star of the new Series E Stutz range. Available with either a four or six-cylinder engine, the Bearcat (below) featured Stutz's patented three-speed gearbox/rear axle unit and could exceed 80mph.

Built near Paris, the Le Zèbre first appeared in 1909 as a 600cc, single-cylinder voiturette, although an 8hp, four-cylinder model was added to the range in 1912, soon followed by a 10/12hp, their first four-seater; this 8hp (bottom) dates from 1914. After the Armistice, the two engineers responsible for the Le Zèbre went on to greater things. Joseph Lamy designed the Amilcar, while Jules Salomon was responsible for the little 5cv Citroën.

1914 Valveless
1914 De Dion-Bouton
1917 Cadillac

Although in later years the name of the David Brown Organisation was to be linked with that of Aston Martin, the famous Huddersfield engineers' first venture into motor manufacture was with the Ralph Lucas-designed Valveless in 1908. The heart of the Valveless was a curious duplex two-stroke engine with 'only six working parts' (two pistons, two con-rods and two crankshafts). The two crankshafts were geared together, running in opposite directions (1914 Valveless 25hp, below).

De Dion-Bouton had dropped the distinctive design of back axle associated with their name in 1911, so this 1914 14hp tourer (left) is fitted with a live axle of conventional type. However, De Dion were still maintaining a technological lead, with the world's first production V8 engine of note, announced in 1910 and still available (latterly with overhead valves) in the early 1920s.

If De Dion pioneered the production V8, it was Cadillac who made it a triumphant reality, with their eight-cylinder unit which appeared in September 1914. Avoiding all the design shortcomings which had bedevilled the De Dion, the Cadillac engine was almost 50% more powerful. The Cadillac car was lavishly equipped, with engine-driven tyre pump, Cadillac's famous electric starting and lighting system, thermostatically controlled cooling system and dipping headlamps. Yet it cost only $2700 in its cheapest form, and Cadillac sold over 13,000 of this model (which remained their sole offering for a decade) in the first year of production, averaging 15,000 annually thereafter. This 1917 landaulette is typical of the early Cadillac V8, a car which inspired the famous advertisement 'The Penalty of Leadership' which confidently upheld Cadillac's claim to be best, despite jealous criticism from their rivals, and which coined a new slogan 'The Standard of the World'.

1918 Pierce-Arrow
1915 Ford
1918 Temperino
1910 Piccard-Pictet
1920 Vauxhall

In 1918, Pierce-Arrow ceased production of the monstrous 66, after that model's most successful year, in which 301 were built. This 1918 tourer is typical of the final form of the Pierce-Arrow 66 (below left), with a 12ft 3½in wheelbase and an engine of 13,514cc, the largest power unit ever fitted to an American production car. In their declining years, many Pierce 66s were converted into chain-driven fire engines; total output of this huge vehicle was 1638, over a span of ten years.

Mass-produced in unprecedented numbers the Model T Ford may have been, but certainly in its pre-1917 brass-radiator form it was not devoid of style. Some Model T variants could be positively elegant, like this 1915 Coupelet (left), 'as convenient and exclusive as an electric'. In 1914–15, Ford sales exceeded 300,000, so all customers were given a $50 rebate as a sales stunt inspired by Henry Ford himself.

One of the more substantial-looking cyclecars was the Temperino, built in Turin. Its Fiat-like radiator shell was only a dummy, though, for the car was powered by an air-cooled, ohv, vee-twin engine of 1100cc, with a kick-starter mounted between the dumbirons. Transmission was odd, for the engine was linked by shaft to a three-speed gearbox mounted in unit with the rear axle, but only the offside wheel was driven. Thus, the Temperino brothers avoided the trouble and expense of a differential unit (1918 model, below left).

The first Piccard-Pictet cars appeared in 1906, the work of a firm of hydraulic engineers from Les Charmilles, near Geneva. Based on the Hispano-Suiza, the cars were sold as SAGs in Switzerland, and as Pic-Pics in Britain. After a reorganisation in 1910, the Pic-Pic name was universal, and in the following year the company adopted the Argyll single-sleeve-valve engine. This is one of the last Pic-Pics to be built, a sleeve-valve, 2950cc 15cv of 1919 (below).

In 1913, a wealthy Stockport businessman, Joseph Higginson, bespoke a hill-climb car from Vauxhall. The result was the prototype of Vauxhall's most famous sports car, the 30/98, a 4.5-litre development of the Prince Henry. Its model designation, incidentally, was apparently an oblique compliment to a rival sporting car, the 38/90 Métallurgique. Shown here (bottom) is a 1920 E-Type side-valve 30/98.

During World War I, Vauxhall built
nearly 2000 cars for the British War
Office. One of these 25hp staff cars
carried General Allenby into
Jerusalem, while another was the
first Allied car to cross the Rhine into
Germany after the Armistice in
November 1918. When King George
V was taken across the Flanders mud
in 1917 to visit Vimy Ridge,
captured by the Allies that April, he
rode in a 25hp Vauxhall, too. Here,
the King, accompanied by General
Sir Arthur Paget, KCB, and General
Stephenson, reviews a battalion of the
Royal Scots.

1921 Hillman
1921 AC
1921 Horstman

One of the best of the Edwardian light cars was the little 9hp Hillman, introduced in 1913; it had a 1357cc engine and sold for £200. A development of this model, the 1496cc Ten, formed the mainstay of Hillman's post-Armistice production (below). The car shown here is flying false colours, as its original short radiator has been replaced by a much deeper Clyno cooler. Hillman also produced a Speed Model Ten, an example of which Raymond Mays used for his Brooklands racing debut.

John Portwine was a butcher, John Weller a talented engineer, and together they founded a company to build the Auto-Carrier, a delivery tricar designed by Weller in 1905. Passenger versions followed in 1907, while the first four-wheeled AC was built in 1913. After the War, S.F. Edge, tiring of his pigs, became a director then Chairman of AC Cars limited. This 1921 tourer (bottom), with a 1496cc Anzani engine and transmission disc brake, dates from 1921.

Built in Bath, the Horstman Super Sports (below) had a 1.4-litre Anzani engine and sold for £500 ready to race. With mild tuning, a Super Sports could be made to exceed 90mph on the track. Production models of the Horstman at that time were fitted with an Archimedian kick-starter with a ferocious reputation. This actual car took part in the 1921 200-Mile race at Brooklands.

92

1921 Minerva
1923 Humber
1921 AV

The Minerva, 'Goddess of Automobiles', was one of the finest cars to be built in Belgium. In 1921, Minerva introduced a magnificent six-cylinder model with sleeve valves, a feature of all Minervas since 1910 (below). With a swept volume of 5340cc, the new Minerva offered silent refinement rather than out-and-out performance. Typically, the instruction book told the chauffeur to replenish the torque tube every 2000 miles with a 'wine-glassful of oil'.

A fine example of the very rare Humber Chummy, as restored by Humber apprentices. This 1923 car (bottom) is powered by a 985cc, overhead-inlet, side-exhaust engine, which produced a respectable 20bhp at 3000rpm; fuel consumption was only 35mpg, however.

Messrs Ward and Avey, of Teddington, Middlesex, were among those optimists who tried to make their fortune out of the unprecedented demand for cars after World War I. The cyclecar they offered an unsuspecting public was based on the pre-war Carden Monocar design, and as crude as could be. Made largely out of wood, the AV Monocar had centre-pivot steering and less than satisfactory weight distribution, for its powerful 8hp, vee-twin engine was mounted at the rear, to the detriment of handling.

1921 Fiat
1922 Phänomobil
1921 GN

One of Fiat's few failures—but a magnificent one—was the Tipo 520 'Superfiat', a 6.8-litre V12 of advanced design, unveiled in 1921. Only a handful of these machines saw the light of day, but the overall design was so promising that Fiat simplified and adapted it for production as the Tipo 519, with a 4.8-litre, six-cylinder engine and massive hydro-mechanical, servo-assisted brake drums on all four wheels. The sporting Tipo 519S version (below) had a handsome vee radiator and flared wings.

A truly curious survival is this Phänomobil, built by a company of cycle makers from Zittau in Germany from 1907 to 1927 in virtually unchanged form. Early models had an air-cooled, vee-twin engine driving the front wheel by chain; from 1912, a transverse four-cylinder engine of 1548cc was used. Relatively popular in its native land because of its economy, the Phänomobil did not travel well; nevertheless, some, like this 1922 example (bottom left), were used as light delivery trucks in England.

One of the best-known and most successful of the cyclecars, the GN survived into the early 1920s, some 3000 having been built in England, and perhaps the same number under licence in France. At one time, a fleet of sixty GNs was used by the commercial travellers of the Cherry Blossom boot polish company; this 1921 GN is a Touring model (below).

1922 Ford
1922 OM
1921 Lancia
1922 Citroën
1922 Detroit Electric

Ford output passed a million in twelve months for the first time in 1922, the year that this Model T touring car (below) was built; in the following year, the two million mark was reached. In fact, this car has most of the characteristics of the 1923 Model T—lower body lines and raked windshield—but lacks the deeper radiator with a fairing at the bottom of the shell of the true 1923 model, announced in August 1922.

The first car to bear the name OM was produced in 1918, and it was a reliable if plain car. The Officine Meccaniche, a huge engineering conglomerate, had absorbed the old Züst company in 1918, and for a while continued with the pre-war S305 model mildly brought up to date. It was, seemingly, an Austrian with the odd name of Barratouché who designed the first 'new' OM, the 1327cc 465, developed into the 1496cc 469 in 1922. This model (bottom) was in production until 1929.

Perhaps the most technically remarkable car of the vintage era was the Lancia Lambda, built in prototype form in 1921, first exhibited to the public in 1922 and in full production the next year (below). It combined a stressed, rigid monocoque body/chassis unit with sliding-pillar independent front suspension and a narrow-angle V4, 2120cc engine, with cast-iron liners in an aluminium block. Maximum speed was over 70mph in touring trim.

André Citroën, who had been chief engineer at Mors, started his own car factory in 1919, building a 10hp tourer in large numbers in premises which had formerly belonged to his old company. In 1922 came the first small Citroën, the Salomon-designed 5cv, nicknamed the *Citron Pressé* (*lemonade*) because of its characteristic yellow paint (bottom centre); it was in production until 1925.

Electric cars lasted longer in America than anywhere else, mainly because a poor road system still kept many motorists within city limits, even in the 1920s, and the limited range of the electric car was therefore not such a hindrance. The Detroit Electric (bottom right) was in production from 1907 to 1942 (latterly only to special order) and, although this 1922 brougham is little changed from pre-war models, later Detroits were disguised to look like petrol cars.

1924 Sima-Violet
1923 Tatra
1923 Calcott

Marcel Violet had been associated with a number of different cyclecars before he launched the Sima-Violet (below left) in 1924. Built at Courbevoie Seine, the Sima-Violet was powered by an air-cooled, 496cc, flat-twin, two-stroke engine mounted on the nose of the car. The marque had some sporting pretensions, although its claimed top speed of 50mph was open to some doubt. Nevertheless, the car's success was assured by its selling price of £57.50 in its native France.

The 65hp Tatra of 1923 was, in fact, a development of the pre-war Nesselsdorf Type U (which had utilised front wheel brakes as early as 1909), and was the work of Hans Ledwinka, (bottom left). Powered by a 6-litre, ohc engine, this was the last Tatra model of conventional design for, once Ledwinka began designing for his old company again, in 1923, he introduced the famous backbone-frame, air-cooled, swing-axle cars.

Calcott Brothers of Coventry, another car company which began life as a cycle manufacturer, made their first car in 1913. This was the famous 'Ten', a refined four-cylinder model which was also produced post-war. Note that its radiator header tank, as depicted on this 1923 11.9hp Calcott (below), is distinctively shouldered. Although the Calcott had a sound reputation, it failed to stand competition from its mass-produced rivals, and the company was taken over by Singer in 1926.

1924 Sénéchal
1924 Peugeot
1924 Sizaire Frères

Robert Sénéchal, born in France in 1892, started building—and racing—voiturettes in 1921. The first Sénéchal had a 904cc, four-cylinder Ruby engine and two-speed gearbox, but in 1922 a three-speed transmission was standardised; in that year, too, the sports Ruby engine of 985cc became available. The 1924 season saw the introduction of this 1095cc Sénéchal Sport, with an ohv Ruby engine, and victory for Robert Sénéchal in the 24-hour Bol d'Or race, a feat repeated in 1926.

This delightful little French cyclecar (below) is the 1924 Peugeot 172BS Grand Sport, derived from the original Quadrilette of 1919, a tandem-seated, 628cc economy car. This car was one of the first Ouadrilettes to have a 719cc power unit. A stripped version of this model won the 750cc class in the Grand Prix MC de Lyon in 1924, driven by one M. Ducreux.

One of the most technically advanced cars of its day, the Sizaire Frères (bottom), introduced in 1924, had all-round independent suspension and a remarkably rigid chassis frame, with a stressed steel undershield adding strength. Front wheel brakes were standard, and pushing the handbrake lever forward applied the front brakes, while pulling it back applied the rear brakes. Power was provided by a 1993cc, ohc, four-cylinder engine.

1924 Opel
1925 Rolls-Royce
1926 Fiat
1925 Duesenberg

Opel were the first German company to build cars on a moving production line (in 1924), and the car which they built, the 4/12PS, was a close copy of the successful 5cv Citroën. Painted bright green, the little Opel was nicknamed *Laubfrosch* (*Tree Frog*), and sold at 4000 marks (about £200). By 1925, the Opel factory at Russelsheim was producing 125 *Laubfrosche* a day, and the model gave the company a dominant 37.5% of the German market by the year 1928 (below).

After nineteen years, the Rolls-Royce Silver Ghost finally went out of production in 1925; its successor, the New Phantom, had a 7668cc, six-cylinder engine, cast in two blocks of three, but with a common cylinder head. Most coachwork on the Phantom was formal, but a very few sporting models were turned out early on (centre left). A total of 2212 Phantoms was built before the Phantom II appeared in 1929.

From 1923, all new Fiat cars were given a road test on a unique test track six stories up on the roof of the company's new factory at Lingotto. Even so, the Fiat 507, developed from the earlier 505 in 1926, was a 2.3-litre car of ponderous character (bottom left). A new feature was the squared-off radiator shell in place of the old pear-shaped cooler.

The original Duesenberg model was the Straight-8, current from 1921 to 1928. It was America's first production straight-eight, and the first to feature hydraulic brakes, three years ahead of the rest of the market. Its valves were operated by a single overhead camshaft, and the power unit, entirely built by Duesenberg in their new Indianapolis factory, made extensive use of aluminium, pioneering the use of alloy pistons in America. This roadster by coachbuilders Millspaugh & Irish represents the 1920s American

concept of a sports car: it has a special locker at the rear to take the owner's golf bag! Advertising of the period claimed 'A Duesenberg is a thing of fineness and precision—a stress-enduring, masterful, mechanical creation—a veritable symphony in steel'.

1923 Morris
1926 Voisin
1925 Delage
1925 Mathis

The car which established Morris as a mass-producer was the Morris Cowley, which first appeared in April 1915, equipped with an American-built Continental Red Seal engine. But the most famous of these 'Bullnose' Cowleys appeared in July 1919, and used a 1548cc engine built by Hotchkiss of Coventry. Between 1919 and 1923, the Cowley (below) had combined head/side lamps mounted on the front mudguards.

Introduced to meet the demand for a high-quality light car which existed in post-Armistice Europe, the Voisin C4 had a 1243cc four-cylinder engine–sleeve-valve, of course!–designed by a young engineer named Marius Bernard, which offered excellent performance but was only rated at eight taxable horsepower in France. This 1924 C4 Berline (bottom left) is from the Dreye Collection.

In 1922, Delage built a prototype sports car based on his successful 2.1-litre Type DE, but fitted with an overhead-valve conversion designed by Henri Toutée which more than doubled the power output to 75bhp. Known as the Type DIS, the new car became one of the best-known vintage sports cars, and over nine hundred examples (including the *surbaissée* Type DISS) were built between 1924 and 1927. This 1925 DIS (bottom centre) carries coachwork by Kelsch.

The first cars to be sold by the Strasbourg-based Mathis company were designed by Ettore Bugatti in 1904, but the marque became best-known for its light cars, like the 1100cc Babylette of the immediate pre-World War I period. This 1925 P-Type has a 1.1-litre, side-valve engine and is fitted with *camionette* bodywork, equally useful for carrying passengers, livestock or vegetables.

1925 AC
1927 Voisin
1924 Turcat-Méry

The most lasting result of S.F. Edge's association with AC cars was the development of a new six-cylinder power unit of advanced design, which remained in production from 1919 to 1963, by which time its output had risen from under 40bhp to 103bhp. Making extensive use of light alloy—block and pistons were both of this material—and with iron wet-liners, the Weller-designed engine also had an overhead camshaft driven by chain. Shown here is a 1925 Aceca coupé.

Aviation pioneer Gabriel Voisin had a profound distaste for non-functional design which manifested itself not only in the highly effective sleeve-valve-engined chassis marketed by his company from 1919 on, but also in the idiosyncratic coachwork with which he, weary of the adipose construction of conventional bodywork, clothed them. Voisin drew on his racing experience in designing his first six-cylinder model, the 1927 C11 (below).

MM Turcat and Méry, of Marseilles, built their first car in 1896, and in 1901 signed an agreement to design the next season's De Dietrich models, an arrangement which provided the pair (who were brothers-in-law) with some much-needed working capital for the continued survival of the Turcat-Méry marque. A Turcat-Méry won the first Monte Carlo Rally in 1911, in which year the link with De Dietrich was broken. In 1924, Turcat-Méry announced the 2.4-litre, ohc Type UG (bottom).

It is debatable whether the Golden Age of cinema comedy would have been so remarkable if used Model T Fords had not been available for instant destruction in front of the cameras. As little as $5 could buy a few-years-old Tin Lizzie, and at one time it seemed that slapstick film makers like Hal Roach and Mack Sennett were writing off Model Ts for laughs almost as fast as Henry Ford was building them. Perhaps the most inventive Lizzie-smashers were Stan Laurel and Oliver Hardy, seen here in a scene from one of their early two-reel talkies, *Hog Wild*, with a Model T that has just become a tram sandwich. In another film, a Model T was sliced into two equal halves by a band-saw . . .

King George V, although a capable driver who frequently took the wheel on his private estates, never drove himself on public roads. For many years, he had the same chauffeur, Humfrey, who was never permitted to exceed 40mph. Like his father Edward VII, George V preferred Daimler cars, and at the end of his reign, in 1936, there were eight Daimlers, all Double-Sixes, in the Royal Garage at Windsor. This picture (below) shows King George and Queen Mary taking delivery of an earlier model in 1924.

Another film star with a distinctive taste in motor cars was Rodolpho Alfonzo Rafaelo Pierre Filibert Guigliemi di Valentina d'Antonguolla (Rudolph Valentino, to the public), whose stable included two Voisins and an Isotta-Fraschini, all endowed with his distinctive cobra mascot. Here (bottom), Valentino poses with one of his Voisins, a 1925 C5.

1925 Frazer Nash
1926 Chevrolet
1927 Rolls-Royce

After leaving GN, Captain Archie Frazer-Nash began to build Frazer Nash cars at Kingston-on-Thames, Surrey, in 1924. Although outwardly a conventional sports car, beneath its aluminium coachwork, the Frazer Nash car concealed the chain-and-dog transmission of its cyclecar forebear. Typical of the breed is this 1925 Anzani-engined Super Sports Three-Seater, which, at a price of £345, offered the performance of a car costing at least twice as much (below).

Reputed to have belonged to film star Greta Garbo, this 1927 Rolls-Royce Phantom I carries sporting boat-tailed coachwork by Barker (right). Access to the rear seat, through the fold-down front passenger seat, would appear to require an agility not usually associated with Rolls-Royce clientele; the aerofoil-section running boards double as tool boxes.

Acquired by General Motors in 1917, Chevrolet became one of America's top-selling models within a remarkably short time. Announced in 1923, the Chevrolet 'Superior' was a direct competitor to the Model T Ford, offering a better specification at a slightly higher price. This 1926 Series V Superior (left) has the Duco cellulose paintwork which made Chevrolet such a colourful alternative to the 'black-is-beautiful' *Tin Lizzie* from Ford.

1926 Clyno
1927 Swift
1926 Rolls-Royce

Clyno of Wolverhampton, originally motor cycle manufacturers, were trading on a fine wartime record when they introduced their first production car, a 10.8hp Coventry Climax-engined model, in 1922. Clyno aimed to rival Morris, and priced their cars accordingly. At their peak, in 1926–27, they were one of Britain's most popular cars, but a costly new factory and a disastrous 8hp model caused their downfall in 1929 (1926 10.8hp, below).

Although Swift of Coventry were aiming at the same market as Clyno, they were hardly in the same league. Originally sewing machine makers, Swift became the first British company to manufacture bicycles, in 1869. Their first car appeared in 1902 and, up to 1914, their range was highly complex. The 1912 10hp model formed the basis of Swift's vintage production, which was always on a modest scale. This is the largest Swift of the 1920s (bottom left), the 1954cc 14/40hp of 1927.

Barker & Company, coachbuilders of
South Audley Street, Mayfair, were
already over two hundred years old
when they built this elegant
aluminium torpedo tourer for his
excellency the Nawab Wali-Ud Dowla
Bahadur, President of Hyderabad
State, India, in 1926. Built on a
Rolls-Royce Phantom I chassis, the
car was used until 1948.

1926 Panhard & Levassor
1926 Pontiac
1926 Citroën
1927 Packard
1927 Lancia

Like Daimler, Panhard & Levassor had a long love affair with the Knight sleeve-valve engine, in the case of the French company dating back to 1911. From 1922 to 1939, every Panhard produced had a sleeve-valve engine, and bore the initials 'SS' (for *sans soupapes*—valveless) on its radiator. Compared with the eccentric styling of the 1930s Panhards, this 1926 2166cc, four-cylinder model (below) was totally conventional, but light steel sleeves gave it a good performance.

They called the Pontiac 'The Chief of the Sixes' when it was launched in 1926 by General Motors as a lower-priced running mate to the Oakland. Before long, Pontiac had supplanted the older marque in the popular estimation and, by 1930, Oakland had vanished from the scene. Pontiac—whose name derives from a mighty Indian chief of the mid 1700s—is the only marque to have been created, rather than acquired, by General Motors which has survived (1926 sedan, bottom left).

In 1925, Citroën were the first European company to put all-steel bodywork into mass production with their new B12 model. Although the rigid coachwork did tend to disagree with the whippy chassis, Citroën persisted, and in 1926 brought out the much-improved B14, with an engine enlarged to 1.5-litres, and four-wheel brakes (bottom centre). By 1928, Citroën were building 100,000 cars a year—half the total French production.

Packard classified their cars by Series, not by model year, so this 1927 Phaeton (below) is a Fifth Series Six Model 526 (5 for the series and 26 for the 126in wheelbase); this was Packard's last six-cylinder range for a decade. A total of 41,750 Fifth Series Sixes was built between 1 July 1927 and 1 August 1928, when the model was replaced by the Standard Eight.

Although it looks little altered from the earlier model shown on page 97, this 1927 Seventh Series Lancia Lambda (above) is, in fact, quite different beneath the surface. Instead of the panelled skeleton chassis, Lancia were now using a single skin stressed hull, with a double thickness of metal below the doors for extra strength, and a larger, wider-angle vee engine of 2370cc, which gave a third more power.

1927 Mercedes-Benz
1926 Rolls-Royce
1926 Pontiac
1929 Fiat
1927 Bugatti

The Mercédès company began experiments with supercharging on aero engines in 1915, and put their first supercharged sports cars into production in 1921. On these blown cars, the supercharger was not operational all the time, only cutting in with a banshee wail when the accelerator pedal was pushed hard down. The early supercharged Mercédès cars proved dangerous, but the 1927 6.3-litre S26/120/180hp Mercedes-Benz (below) was, perhaps, Germany's finest sports car, winning 53 races in 1928.

More formal coachwork on the Rolls-Royce Pantom I chassis (bottom left). This landaulette was built by Hooper, another coachbuilder whose experience dated back to the days of the horse-drawn carriage. The spun aluminium wheel discs were common wear on Rolls-Royce cars, as they saved the chauffeur the thankless task of cleaning the wire-spoked wheels.

In the first year of production, Pontiac sold 76,742 of their $825 3-litre six cars, and nearly doubled this figure the following year. This 1926 coupé (bottom centre) is surprisingly elegant for so cheap a car. The designer of the Pontiac, Ben H. Anibal, was a former chief engineer with Cadillac.

Introduced in 1928, the 3.7-litre Fiat 525 was the first car from the Torinese colossus to be fitted with hydraulic brakes. Could this elegant Coupé d'Orsay (below) be the very car presented personally to the Pope in 1929 by Giovanni Agnelli, head of Fiat?

Developed from Bugatti's first straight-eight, the Type 28 of 1922, the 3-litre Type 44 first appeared in 1927. In chassis form, the Type 44 cost 60,000 francs (then equivalent to around £550). Equally suitable for sporting or formal coachwork such as this four-light saloon (bottom right), the Type 44 was capable of around 80mph in touring trim.

1927 OM
1928 Pierce-Arrow
1927 Humber

Aptly named Superba, the Type 665 OM of 1927 (below) had a 1991cc, side-valve engine with a remarkable turn of speed. Two of these machines finished equal fourth overall in the 1924 Le Mans, only 4mph slower than the winning Lorraine's 57.8mph, while another averaged 103.57kph for six days and nights at the Monza autodrome at the end of 1927 to set up a new 15,000km record.

'By their headlights shall ye know them', was the implicit marketing policy of Pierce-Arrow, whose distinctive fender headlamps were an instant identifying feature. But for the 1928 Series 81 Runabout (bottom), stylist James R. Way threw conservatism to the winds and not only went in for Art Deco colour schemes, but also committed the appalling solecism of putting the Pierce name on the radiator. Poor sales soon forced the Series 81 off the market.

Staunchly middle-class, the vintage Humber cars were solidly engineered to give decades of faithful service. External-contracting front-wheel brakes first appeared in 1925, but, by the time that this 1927 14/40hp Doctor's Coupé was built, safer drum front stoppers had been adopted. The 1927 season saw 4000 Humbers sold, but that was not good enough to compete against the mass-producers, and Humber were soon absorbed into the Rootes Group.

Two stars with but a single car—a 1928 model Buick Six Sport Sedan, obviously used as studio transport at Paramount, where Emil Jannings (in period dress, upper photo) was one of the leading actors of the silent era. In 1928, Jannings was awarded the Academy Award for the best performance of the year, already aware that his Hollywood career was finished, since the advent of talkies had revealed his heavy German accent. Below is another actor, William Jacobs.

Alfonso XIII of Spain, had a most catholic taste in motor cars. Although his name is most often linked with that of Hispano-Suiza, at various times the Royal stables also included examples of Panhard, ReVere and, in the late 1920s, Model A Ford. In exile in Paris in 1932, the King drove one of the new Ford V8 cars. Here, Alfonso XIII rides in a blown Mercedes-Benz of 1927 vintage.

1928 Stutz
1928 Mercedes-Benz
1928 Bean
1928 Oméga-Six

The Stutz Vertical Eight was the sensation of the 1926 New York Auto Show. Designed by Paul Bastien, late of Métallurgique of Belgium, the new Stutz was low-built, with both speed and safety in mind. Its 4.7-litre engine had a single overhead camshaft and hydraulic four-wheel brakes were standard. Fastest of all the 'Splendid Stutz' models was the Black Hawk Speedster (1928 model, below), an example of which gave Bentley a close run in the 1928 Le Mans, finishing second.

The Mercedes-Benz Nürburg 460 of 1928 had a straight-eight, overhead-camshaft engine of 4.6 litres, and the American-inspired styling which was so popular in the Germany of the late 1920s, including the odd combination of knock-on wood wheels with detachable rims (bottom left). Like the S26/120/180hp (page 114), the Nürburg was designed by Dr Ferdinand Porsche, who left Daimler-Benz in January 1929 to join Steyr in Austria.

On its way out in 1928, the 14/40 Bean (below) was the final development of a theme introduced in 1923. Alongside this strong and reliable machine, Bean offered another type of 14/40 of entirely new design, which cost more and was therefore more heavily taxed. Such an eccentric marketing policy presaged disaster and, sure enough, Bean cars were off the market by the end of the 1929 season.

If it had been better financed, the Oméga-Six from Boulogne-sur-Seine could have been a rival to the Hispano-Suiza. Beautifully made, the Oméga-Six had a single-overhead-camshaft engine of great refinement. Early examples—the marque made its debut at the 1922 Paris Salon—had a 2-litre engine. By the time this 1928 model (bottom right) appeared, the Oméga-Six had acquired a 2914cc engine, developing over 120bhp enabling the car to reach 106mph. By 1930, however, Oméga-Six were out of business.

1928 Packard
1928 Packard
1929 Volvo

Packard's Fifth Series Six Convertible Coupé first went into production on 1 January 1928. This particular example (below) is fitted with the optional side-mounted spare wheels and cowl lamps which made this car a smaller replica of the contemporary eight-cylinder Packards. During the 1928 season, Packard sales reached a total of 50,000 for the first time.

'Volvo' is Latin for 'I roll', a doubly appropriate name for this company from Gothenburg, Sweden, founded in 1927 with financial backing from the SKF ball-bearing company. Their first offering was the 1.9-litre, four-cylinder P4, a well preserved example of which can sometimes be seen in the streets of Gothenburg. In 1929 came the first six-cylinder Volvo (right), the 3-litre PV651, a solid-looking machine on American lines.

The introduction of the Sixth Series Eight, on 1 August 1928, saw Packard committed to an eight-cylinders-only policy. Typical of the breed is this 1928 645 Phaeton, (left) which came with a choice of seven different final-drive ratios and a wide range of options from an onyx horn button at $1.85 to a monogrammed lap robe at $115. The gold-plated *cloisonné* enamel radiator emblem carried the pelican crest of Samuel Packard, who landed in America in 1638.

1929 Rosengart
1929 Essex
1929 MG

Another licence-built version of the Austin Seven, the Rosengart was built at Neuilly-sur-Seine from 1928. It differed from its English prototype mainly in matters of styling, although the engineer employed by Lucien Rosengart was none other than Jules Salomon, who had helped create the first Citroën. Despite their subsequent ventures into front-wheel drive, Rosengart remained faithful to the Austin theme until 1939 and, indeed, were still using the 747cc Austin engine in some 1952 models.

Introduced in 1918 as a lower-priced running mate to the Hudson line, the Essex was one of the first American makes to announce a cheap closed model, the two-door 'coach' of 1920. From 1924, Essex cars were powered by a lively six-cylinder engine, and the model helped to push the Hudson-Essex group into third place in the US market by 1929, in which year this Super Six Speedabout (below) was just one of the 300,962 cars built in their Detroit factory.

Britain's first cheap production sportscar was the MG Midget, which first appeared in 1929 (bottom), derived from the Morris Minor. Despite its humble origins, the MG Midget was a lively little vehicle and, in 1930, the model took the team prize in the Brooklands Double-Twelve Race. This is the standard fabric-covered two-seater Midget; in 1931, a Midget-based blown record-breaker became the smallest car in the world to achieve 100mph.

1929 Hispano-Suiza
1929 Pontiac
1929 Lincoln
1929 Chevrolet
1929 Mercedes-Benz

Kellner of Paris built the luxurious coupé body on this 1929 37.2hp Hispano-Suiza (below) to the order of the Maharajah of Alwar, as a wedding present for his son. The equipment included Grebel searchlights on telescopic arms attached to the running board, for use when hunting big game at night. The bell in front of the radiator was for frightening natives out of the Hispano's path!

In 1929, the Pontiac was redesigned, with many features in common with the recently introduced Marquette range, including a 3277cc, six-cylinder engine. The radiators were similar, too, except that the Pontiac bore a stylised Indian head as a mascot. The Marquette failed to last beyond 1931, however, while the Pontiac (1929 landaulette, bottom) stayed the course.

The Lincoln company, founded by Henry M. Leland after he left Cadillac, was taken over by Ford in 1922, and the cars were injected with some much-needed style by the gifted Edsel Ford. Originally equipped with a 5.8-litre, V8 engine, the Lincoln acquired a 6.3-litre power unit in 1928. The finest coachbuilders in America clothed the Lincoln chassis; this 1929 Club Roadster (below right) is bodied by Locke.

Popularly known as the 'Cast Iron Wonder' or 'Stove Bolt Six', Chevrolet's famous ohv, six-cylinder engine was given its first public showing on New Year's Day, 1929. With a swept volume of 3.2 litres, the six-cylinder engine was to remain in production until 1953; output during the first year was 1,328,605, a record unsurpassed until 1941. Most of the new Chevys wore disc wheels, but this pretty 1929 Sport Coupé (centre right) wears the non-standard wire type.

The apogee of the Porsche-designed supercharged Mercedes line was the 38/250SS of 1929 (bottom right), which gave shattering performance, even on the roads of the late 1920s. Its 7.1-litre, six-cylinder engine would pull a 2.76:1 top gear, and a touring 38/250SS like this one, specially built for Lord Cholmondeley, could achieve an indicated 120mph with the blower in operation. A similar car won the 1929 Ulster TT at 72.82mph.

talking picture *Men of Steel*, as a
status symbol to show his rise from
steel worker to executive. Aimed at
the upper-middle-class bracket, the
Buicks of the late 1920s were
handsomely styled. Four-wheel brakes
had been a Buick feature since 1924.

They had called the Oakland the car 'built for the man who demands proof', and movie star 'bad man' Fred Kohler seems quite happy with what his All-American Six of 1929 has just proved to him. Fred is about to drive the car onto a Paramount set in Hollywood (below).

More Hollywood glamour, this time from the Fox studios. Stars Nick Stuart and Sue Carol in a 1929 Cadillac with a distinctly sporty body by Fleetwood, with such classic touches as two-tone paint, side-mounted spare wheel and fold-flat windscreen with side-wings (bottom).

1929 Riley
1929 Lea-Francis
1929 Bentley

When it was announced in 1926, the 1088cc Riley Nine caused a sensation, for its lively overhead-valve power unit was capable of propelling it at speeds of over 60mph. At the end of 1927 came the stylish Monaco fabric saloon, which soon became the most popular version of this car, offering sports car performance and saloon car comfort. at the modest price of £298—which was maintained until the Monaco went out of production in 1938! Open Nines (below) were uncommon.

Faced with a demand for a bigger Bentley, in 1926 W.O. Bentley brought out a new 6½-litre model which, although eventually developed into the magnificent Speed Six of 1929, initially disappointed the Bentley clientele. Steam wagon builder Foden said that his 6½-litre lacked the 'bloody thump' of his beloved 3-litre Bentley. So, in 1927, the 4½-litre Bentley (right) was born. In standard trim, it could exceed 90mph, and a 4½-litre won the 1928 Le Mans.

Another supercharged sports car of the late 1920s was the 1929 Lea-Francis Hyper, which had a 1½-litre Meadows engine with a Cozette blower (left). This particular car is a replica of that in which Kaye Don won the 1928 Ulster Tourist Trophy race at 64.06mph, receiving both the *Daily Mail* Trophy and *The Motor's* prize for the 1½-litre class. Top speed of the Hyper was around 90mph, and the car represented too good a value for money at only £495. Small wonder that Lea-Francis were forced into receivership in November 1930.

1929 Alfa-Romeo
1929 Swallow
1929 BMW

Introduced in 1929, the 1750cc Alfa Romeo, designed by Vittorio Jano, remained in production until 1934. This is the Super Sport version (below), with a supercharged, twin-overhead-camshaft engine, capable of around 95mph. This model enjoyed considerable competition success, including victories in the Mille Miglia in 1929 and 1930 and in the Belgian 24 hours race; Nuvolari drove one to first place in the 1930 Tourist Trophy, too.

The Austin Seven was, in its usual guise, a basic and boxy vehicle, but the Swallow Sidecar and Coachbuilding Company clothed it in bulbous bodywork designed by William Lyons. They had just moved from Blackpool to Foleshill, near Coventry, in late 1928 when they introduced the Swallow Saloon on the Austin chassis (bottom); similar bodies were provided for Swift, Fiat and Standard. Swallow, later SS, became Jaguar in 1945.

BMW began as aircraft manufacturers
during World War I, but by 1923
this Bavarian company had moved
into motor-cycle production, with
their famous opposed-cylinder design.
Their first motor-car appeared in
1928 as a result of BMW acquiring
the Dixi company and the rights to
build the Dixi light car, which was
itself a licence-built version of the
Austin Seven. Over 25,000 BMW
Dixis were built up to 1932, and the
model took the team prize in the
1929 Alpine Rally.

1928 Duesenberg
1930 Packard
1930 Buick
1930 Hispano-Suiza
1930 Talbot

Announced at the New York Show in December 1928, the Model J Duesenberg offered a degree of performance unique in a luxury car, a claimed power output of 265bhp from a 6.9-litre straight eight, giving 89mph in second gear and 116mph in top..Some 470 examples of the J and its supercharged derivative, the SJ, were built before the marque went down with the foundering Auburn-Cord-Duesenberg combine in 1937. The J (below) had a chassis price of $8500 (£1700).

A further stage in the development of the Packard was the Seventh Series (Model 740 Custom Phaeton, bottom left), which was built between August 1929 and August 1930. The stamina of this model was proved in 1931 when one of the marque's many royal owners, Prince Eugene de Ligne of Belgium, took a brace of 740s from Brussels to the Belgian Congo across the Sahara Desert. Incidentally, American presidents from Taft to Truman rode in Packards.

The two basic Buicks of the latter half of the 1920s were the Standard and Master Sixes, which were replaced by a range of straight-eights in 1931. In its last year of production, the Master Six (bottom centre) had a 5.1-litre engine—with overhead valves, like all Buicks since plumber David Dunbar Buick founded the line in 1903—external-contracting brakes on all four wheels and detachable rims.

Final incarnation of the 37.2hp Hispano-Suiza was the Type H6C, built between 1928 and 1931, when it was succeeded by the legendary V12 model. This 1930 H6C (below) has an unusual sedanca de ville body by Henri Binder of Paris, with a sliding sunshine roof—a feature, incidentally, invented before World War I by another famous Parisian carrossier, Labourdette.

Although they were produced by the same group, Talbots from Paris and Talbots from London had precious little in common (and in fact the French version was known as the Darracq in the British Commonwealth). This is the Talbot/Darracq from Suresnes, Paris, a 14hp M75 two-seater *avec spider* (with dickey seat), one of the wide range of six-cylinder models offered by Talbot in 1930 (bottom).

1930 **Bugatti**
1930 **Alfa Romeo**
1929 **Delage**
1932 **Duesenberg**
1930 **Citroën**

One of the best of the touring Bugatti chassis was the Type 49, current from 1930 to 1934. Derived from the 1927 Type 44, the Type 49 had a 3.3-litre-straight-eight engine, with two spark plugs per cylinder (below). Its elegant aluminium wheels are similar to those used on Bugatti's huge 12.8-litre La Royale. Bugatti weathered the Depression by building 120mph rail-cars powered by La Royale engines.

The Vittorio Jano-designed 1750 Alfa Romeo was introduced in 1929, and this 1930 drophead coupé (centre left) is one of its rarer manifestations, the Gran Turismo, with an unblown, twin-overhead-camshaft engine, which developed some 55bhp, giving the car a top speed of around 80mph. This particular car was one of the stars of the first International Rally for pre-1940 Alfas, held in Lombardy in 1966.

One of the most consistently elegant marques was Delage, established in 1905 by Louis Delage, a one-eyed engineer from Cognac. Perhaps the finest Delage of all was the D8, designed by Maurice Gaultier and announced at the 1929 Paris Salon. This 1929 Grand Sport Torpedo is bodied by Henri Chapron, and its straight-eight engine has a swept volume of 4050cc. This was the largest version of the D8, with a wheelbase of 11ft 11in in road trim (bottom left).

Many of the classic designs, like the Model J Duesenberg, were carried over into the 1930s from the vintage era. This 1932 Duesenberg, with convertible coupé body by Murphy, is in fact the SJ version, with a centrifugal supercharger running at five times engine speed, and giving a 0-100mph time of 17 secs through the gears. Top speed was claimed to be in the region of 130mph. Price of this model was in the region of $13,500 (below).

Tout Acier, 1930-style (bottom). The 1930 Citroën Familiale has Budd all-steel bodywork on the C6 chassis, a 2½-litre six-cylinder derivative of the B14. This was the first Citroën six, launched in 1928; Citroën's collaboration with Budd dated from 1924, and was a prime factor in the decision to develop the revolutionary *traction avant* Citroën which appeared in 1934.

1930 Bugatti
1931 Ford
1930 Du Pont

Unkindly perhaps, the Type 40 Bugatti of 1926 was dubbed the 'Molsheim Morris-Cowley', but then this 1.5-litre, four-cylinder was—relatively—the most prosaic of the vintage Bugattis. In 1930, the Type 40A appeared, with a larger 1.63-litre power unit. This two-seater roadster (below) has very American styling—compare it with the Ford below—right down to the golf bag locker in the tail.

Another 'transitional' design, the Model A Ford replaced the Model T at the end of 1927, and was produced until 1932. The coloured steel insert in the radiator header identifies this two-seater as a 1931 model. Its bodywork is slightly different from the standard Model A pattern, as this is a German-built car. (bottom), probably from the newly opened Cologne Ford works.

Another American make which proved its worth at Le Mans, the Du Pont was an exclusive car built by the super-rich Du Pont family in Pennsylvania between 1920 and 1932. Output was deliberately limited, and only 537 Du Ponts were built in all. From the mid 1920s, the marque featured hydraulic brakes and a constant-mesh gearbox, and was renowned for its silence. This 1930 Model G Royal Town Car carries coachwork by Merrimac, and has a 5.3-litre, straight-eight engine.

1929 Isotta-Fraschini

Pure Sunset Boulevard! Norma (Gloria Swanson) Desmond's huge car in that 1950 Hollywood classic was an Isotta-Fraschini similar to this 1929 Tipo 8A Farina landaulette de ville. It was an appropriate choice, for several real-life Hollywood stars, including Rudolph Valentino and 'IT' girl Clara Bow, were Isotta owners in the late 1920s. The Tipo 8A originally appeared in 1924, a faster, 7.4-litre version of the original Tipo 8 of 1919, which had a straight-eight engine of 6 litres capacity. Designed by Giustino Cattaneo, the Tipo 8

Isotta was the first straight-eight to go into series production anywhere in the world, although one-off cars with this engine configuration had been built by various makers; the French CGV company, for instance, constructed the first-ever straight-eight as early as 1902.

1929 Isotta-Fraschini
1931 Lancia
1932 Lincoln

Another 1929 Isotta-Fraschini, this time with wire instead of wooden wheels and bodywork by Cesare Sala. This actual car was used as a demonstrator by the London Branch of Isotta-Fraschini, and cost around £2800 complete (below). As far back as 1909, Isotta had been the first maker to standardise four-wheel brakes, and mechanical servo assistance was added on the Tipo 8; another advanced feature was the use of a central gear lever.

Introduced in 1931, the Lancia Artena (bottom left) was intended as a replacement for the Lambda. Like its predecessor, it had a narrow V4 engine, but with a smaller swept volume of 1925cc. The engine was flexibly mounted in rubber and coil spring bearers, giving notably smooth running. However, the Artena was overshadowed by its more popular sister, the V8 Astura 2.6-litre, introduced at the same time. Sales were so poor that it was withdrawn during 1933.

In 1932, Ford introduced their V8 and, not to be outdone, Ford's luxury car company, Lincoln, went four better and announced the KB V12 (bottom right), one of only seven V12 models available on the American market. The 7.2-litre KB chassis normally carried some of the finest American coachwork, but this perpendicular Rollston limousine lacks the classic proportions usually associated with the model.

1932 Delage
1932 Duesenberg
1932 Wolseley
1934 Lagonda

Some of the most fashionable French coachwork of the early 1930s was fitted to the Delage D8 chassis. This handsome Fernandez coupé de ville (below) dates from 1932. Delage sales were hit by the depression, however, and, although Louis Delage tried to save his company, by 1935 it was in receivership. The Delage name did survive, however, although on cars built by Delahaye who acquired the remains of the Delage company after the liquidation.

The design of the Duesenberg SJ changed little between its introduction in 1932 and the end of production in 1937. This LaGrande Dual Cowl 'Sweep Panel' Phaeton (bottom) dates from 1932, but was obviously updated a few years later, for the skirted front wings with which it is now fitted did not become available until 1935. Only 470 or so J and SJ Duesenbergs were built, and the last car was delivered in 1938, after the factory had closed down.

'When the Wolseley Hornet was first planned, the inspiration was to provide the equivalent of first-class express travel in a small car for the first time,' wrote *The Autocar* in 1931, announcing the new Hornet Special sports chassis, a 'most seductive motor car'. In fact, the Hornet started life as a six-cylinder, 1271cc version of the Morris Minor with a rather whippy frame; the Hornet Special (below) was only supplied in chassis form to the builders of sporting bodywork.

A much nicer small sporting car of the early 1930s was the Lagonda Rapier (bottom), which had an 1100cc, four-cylinder engine with twin overhead camshafts. It appeared for the first time in 1934, costing only £270 in chassis form; after the Lagonda company was reformed in 1935, Rapiers were made by a separate firm at Hammersmith, and a supercharged version was announced in 1936. Total production, by the time the last Rapier was built in 1940, had amounted to some 300 cars.

1933 Lancia
1934 Steyr
1931 Alvis
1935 Duesenberg
1932 Rolls-Royce

Lancia's first unitary construction saloon car was the Augusta, (below left) of 1933, which was normally seen with pillarless four-seater saloon coachwork, although a drophead version was also available. Its 1196cc, narrow V4 engine was good for around 70mph, at the expense of a 24mpg petrol consumption. Famous racing driver Tazio Nuvolari used an Augusta as his everyday transport.

Austrian economy (centre left): the Type 100 Steyr, built between 1934 and 36, was a cheap 1.4-litre car with remarkable fuel consumption.

One of the most famous vintage sports cars was the 12/50 Alvis, introduced in 1923, with a 1500cc, ohv power unit of Alvis manufacture. The design was developed through the 1920s, but, apart from increases in bore size, few changes were made. Sports versions of the 12/50 had a 1500cc engine while, from 1926, tourers had a 1645cc power unit. In March 1931 came the twin-carburettor 12/60 sports (bottom left) with the 1645cc engine, shown here with Cross & Ellis beetleback two-seater coachwork.

One of the most desirable body styles available on the Duesenberg SJ was the two-seater roadster (below). This roadster, dating from around 1935, is on the standard short chassis of 11ft 10½in, but in 1936 came the rarest SJ variant of all—the SSJ, with a 10ft 5in wheelbase. Just two SSJ roadsters were built, one for Gary Cooper and one for Clark Gable.

Current between 1929 and 1936, the 20/25hp Rolls-Royce was a 3699cc development of the original light-six Rolls-Royce, the 3127cc 20hp introduced in 1920. Top gear range of the 20/25 was 3mph to 75mph, at a fuel consumption of 15–17mpg. Total production of 20/25s was 3827, over twice as many as the contemporary 7668cc Phantom II. Shown here (bottom right) is an unusual sporting coupé built in 1932.

1935 Ford
1930 Cadillac
1932 SS
1935 MG

Developed in Dearborn for the European market, the 933cc Model Y Ford was the last significant model in whose gestation Henry Ford himself played a part. The first drawings were committed to paper in October 1931, sixteen prototypes were ready for exhibition by mid February 1932 and the Model Y was in full production by August of that year. This Model Y (below) dates from late 1935, when a fully equipped Model Y Tudor cost £100—the only saloon car ever sold at so low a price.

The first and most successful V16 car ever to go into production was the Cadillac, announced in January 1930 (1932 sedanca de ville bottom). Designed by Ernest Seaholm, it had a 7.4-litre, ohv power unit, developing 184bhp, mounted in a specially designed chassis on a 148in wheelbase. All coachwork was by Cadillac's exclusive *carrossier*, Fleetwood, and 3863 V16s were delivered before a new V16 (of which only 511 were to be built) was announced in 1938.

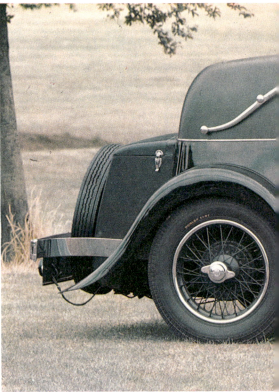

It was exaggerated styling which sold the SS car, built on a specially modified Standard chassis by the Swallow Coachbuilding Company, of Coventry, who had started life making sidecars in a Blackpool garage. The original SS I of 1931, 'long, low and rakishly sporting', was an instant success, although the wilder excesses of its styling had been somewhat toned down by the time that this coupé (below) was built in 1932. Out of the SS grew one of the great cars of motoring history, the Jaguar.

Typical of the MG sports cars of the 1930s and 1940s is this 1935 PB (bottom), introduced at that year's Motor Show. With a 939cc engine, engine, the PB was a development of the 847 P-type of 1934, itself a refined version of the 1932 J-Type Midget. Again, it was styling which sold the little MGs for, although they had good acceleration and road-holding, they were not particularly fast in a straight line.

1934 Riley
1933 Morgan
1934 Hudson
1935 SS

The Riley Nine was, said enthusiastic owner Raymond Mays, 'a really thoroughbred car in which the full meaning of the word "thoroughbred" plays a greater part than in any car I know'. However, by the mid 1930s, the saloon Rileys had put on extra weight at the expense of performance: this 1934 Monaco (below) has steel-panelled coachwork instead of the fabric of the original Monaco. Although it was no longer faster than most of its contemporaries, the Monaco was still a strikingly handsome car.

Representing the ultimate stage in the development of the Morgan three-wheeler, this 1933 Super Sports (bottom) has a front-start, ohv, 1100cc JAP engine mounted in the M-Type chassis, announced in 1930. Much lowered, like the old Brooklands Super Sports, the new chassis had detachable wheels all round and a three-speed gearbox with single chain final drive, rather than the fixed wheels and twin-ratio chain-and-dog transmission of the vintage Morgan three-wheelers.

Virtually indistinguishable from its lower-priced running mate, the Terraplane, this Hudson Convertible Coupé dates from 1934 (below). Powered by a 3½-litre, six-cylinder engine, it developed 80bhp. Hudson/Terraplane sales for 1934 totalled 85,835, more than double the previous year's total, but failed to prevent the Hudson Motor Car Company from recording a loss of $3.25 million.

In 1935, the first SS sports car, the SS90, appeared (bottom), with a six-cylinder, 2.7-litre Standard 20 power unit in a special 104 in wheelbase chassis. The '90' in its name suggested—perhaps a little optimistically—the designed top speed. The SS90 sold for only £395, but was a transitional design. Just fifty had been built when it was replaced by the meretricious SS100.

1933 **Aston Martin**
1935 **Triumph**
1934 **Talbot**
1935 **Daimler**
1934 **BMW**

Although they were constantly bedevilled by financial problems, during the 1920s and 1930s, Aston Martin produced some of the finest sports cars of their day. This 1933 Le Mans Aston dates from 1933 (below), and features the 1495cc, ohc engine designed by A.C. Bertelli, who revived the Aston Martin company in 1926. The twin-carburettor, dry-sump Le Mans engine was good for 84mph in standard form; the exhaust system is non-standard. 1933 was Aston's best sales year when 105 cars were sold.

The Southern Cross (bottom) was a sports version of the 1935 Triumph Gloria, a range of cars named after a glamour girl of the day. Built on an 8ft wheelbase, the Gloria was available with a four-cylinder 1232cc engine or a six-cylinder 1991cc power unit.

One of the outstanding chassis of the 1930s was the Talbot 105 designed by Swiss-born Georges Roesch, and introduced in 1931. It had an ohv, 2970cc, six-cylinder power unit and was available with a wide range of bodywork, from four-seater sports to saloon (1934 model, below right). In its competition form, the 105 scored an enviable list of victories, although a preselector gearbox muted the performance of post-1933 models. In 1935, Rootes acquired Talbot, with the inevitable loss of individuality.

Preselector transmission was used on Daimlers of the 1930s, too, in conjunction with the 'Fluid Flywheel' torque convertor, giving an ease of control unrivalled until the advent of the automatic gearbox. Typical of the wide range of Daimler models of the 1930s is this 1935 15hp, with a 2.5-litre, six-cylinder engine (centre right); this design was revived after the war as the DB18.

BMW's 1934 315/1 Sport (bottom right) was the marque's first truly successful competition car, with a 1490cc, six-cylinder engine which, in triple-carburettor form, developed 40bhp. Its distinctive styling was widely copied by more prosaic machinery, like the 1172cc Ford Eifel produced at Ford's Cologne factory.

1935 Auburn
1935 Cord
1934 Hispano-Suiza

The first fully equipped American stock car to cover over 1200 miles in twelve hours was an Auburn 851 Speedster driven by Ab Jenkins, the 'Mormon Meteor', on the Bonneville Salt Flats in 1935. Designed by Gordon Buehrig, the straight-eight Auburn had a Duesenberg-devised centrifugal supercharger installation, and every Speedster (below) carried a plaque stating that it had been tested at over 100mph before delivery. However, the glamorous—and impractical—Speedster came too late to save Auburn from collapse.

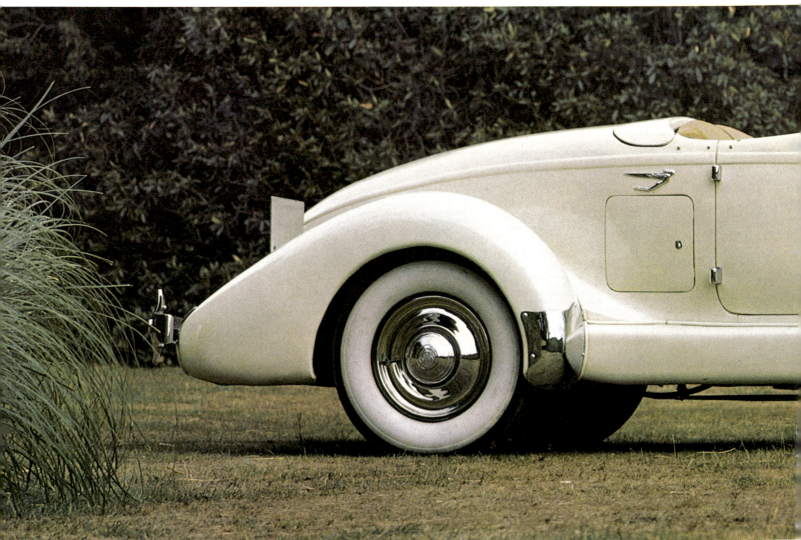

Gordon Buehrig's other classic design for the Auburn-Cord-Duesenberg group was the 'coffin-nose' Cord 810 of 1935, a design so radical that Buehrig patented it. Key features were the wrap-around louvres which replaced the conventional radiator grilles and the retractable headlights (adapted from aircraft landing lights supplied by another component of Erret Lobban Cord's business empire). The 810 (bottom left) was also the first American production car to combine front-wheel drive with independent front suspension.

The largest and most magnificent luxury car to be produced during the 1930s was the V12 Hispano-Suiza, which first appeared in 1931 with a 9424cc power unit, uprated during 1934 to 11,310cc. The wondrously extravagant car shown here (bottom right) is a 1934 example of the 11.3-litre Type 68 bis with two-seater drophead coupé body by Saoutchik, and an overall length of some twenty feet! The last V12 Hispano was built in 1938; after the war, Hispano experimented with a Ford-engined fwd car, but soon abandoned it.

Index

Acknowledgments

Arch. Quattroruote: 21b, 22, 24c, 30b, 45b, 50a, 51b, 52b, 53b, 65b, 66a, b, 68a, 69a, 80b, 81b, 88b, 90a, 91b, 92a, 94/95, 104a, 106a, b, 107a, 112/113, 123a, 124, 125b, 144, 145a, 149b, 150a, 155c—Belli: 9b, 16a, b, 17, 37b, 40a, 41a, b, 46a, b, 51a, 52a, 53c, 58a, b, 64a, b, 65c, 74b, 82b, 84a, b, 85a, 91c, 92b, 100b, 104b, 108a, b, 114a, b, 117a, b, 122b, c, 123b, 124c, 124/125a, 126/127, 146a, 148b, 149a, 154b—Boschetti: 18a, 60b, 68b, 69b, 90b, 94a, 97b, 104/105, 105a, b, 122a, 124b, 126b, 142/143, 144/145, 147a, 152c, 153b, 155b—N. Bruce: 73a, 74a, 85b, 89, 100a, 121, 151b, 152a, 152b—Camera Press: 91a—Ceci: 97a—Cherrett: 16c, 102a—Fiat: 24a, 37a—Hamilton: 126a—ICP: 30a, 40b, 120b, 150b—IMS: 49a, 60a, 78a, 116, 120a, 153a, 156—Italfoto: 49b, 77a—London Art Tech: 26/27—Mansell Collection: 43a—Marka: 67, 81a, 94b, 147b—National Motor Museum: 9a, 10/11, 11a, b, 14, 22/23, 27, 28/29, 29a, b, 31, 33a, 35a, b, 40/41, 42, 43b, 44/45, 54, 55a, b, c, 59, 65a, 70a, b, 70/71, 73b, 77b, 78b, 86/87, 88a, 98/99, 99a, b, 102b, 106/107, 110a, b, 111, 118/119, 119a, b, 125b, 146b—Opel: 94c—Orbis: 13b, 15, 19, 20, 21, 24b, d, 25, 32, 39, 45a, 46/47, 48, 50/51a, b, 53, 56/57a, b, 61, 62/63, 66c, 72, 74/75, 76/77, 78/79, 80a, 82a, 83, 92/93, 96/97, 101, 102/103, 108/109, 112, 113a, 115, 116/117, 117c, 148c, 151a, 154a, 155a, 156/157, 157—Renault: 18b—Tony Stone Assoc: 34, 36, 38—Von Fersen: 13a—J. Spencer-Smith/Orbis: ii/iii, cover—Camera Press: iv—L.J. Caddell/ Orbis: vii—National Motor Museum: endpapers, back cover